PROGRESSIVE

Guitar Method

Notes, Chords & Rhythms

Book 1

BEGINNER

by Gary Turner & Peter Gelling

PROGRESSIVE GUITAR METHOD BOOK 1: NOTES, CHORDS AND RHYTHMS
I.S.B.N. 978-982-9118-03-5
Order Code: 11803

For more information on
this series contact:
L.T.P. Publishing Pty Ltd
email: info@learntoplaymusic.com
or visit our website:
www.learntoplaymusic.com

Published by
KOALA MUSIC PUBLICATIONS ™

Contents

● *Introduction*   **8**
  Guitar Types...11
  Seating, Standing, Using the Pick 13
  Right Arm Position 14
  Left Hand Placement.................................14
  The Rudiments of Music 15
  Count, Pick and Fingering Symbols 17

● **LESSON 1**
  First String Notes......................................19
  Right Hand Support 20
  Pick Technique 20

● **LESSON 2**
  Second String Notes 21
  Song of Joy (Part One)...........................22
  Skip to My Lou......................................22
  Steps and Skips 22

● **LESSON 3**
  The C Major Chord 23
  Strumming..23
  The Seventh Chord 24
  The Half Note Strum..................................24
  Chord Progressions 25
  Pivot Finger 25
  Rhythm Patterns.......................................26
  Open Chord Shapes 26

● **LESSON 4**
  12 Bar Blues 27
  12 Bar Blues in the Key of G 27
  The Whole Note 28
  2 String Blues 28

● **LESSON 5**
  Third String Notes.....................................29
  The Octave 29
  G Major Chord 30
  Slide Finger..30
  Cycling in G 30
  Three String Blues 31
  Guitar Boogie 31

● **LESSON 6**
  Eighth Note Rhythms.................................32
  12 Bar Blues 33
  The Lead-In..33
  Michael Row the Boat Ashore.................33

● **LESSON 7**
  A Major Chord 34
  E Major Chord 34
  D Major Chord 35

● **LESSON 8**
  12 Bar Blues and Seventh Chords 36
  E Seventh Chord 36
  A Seventh Chord 37
  Bluesy Suzie 38
  Aura Lee 38
  Note Summary 39

● **LESSON 9**
  Minor Chords 40
  The Three Four Time Signature 41
  Three Four Time Rhythm Patterns.................41
  Bass Note Rhythm Pattern..........................43

● **LESSON 10**
  Fourth String Notes 44
  The Dotted Half Note 44
  The Dotted Half Strum 44
  Molly Malone 45
  The Tie 46
  Will the Circle Be Unbroken 46
  Walkin' Blues..46
  Note Summary 47

● **LESSON 11**
  Fifth String Notes......................................48
  Volga Boatman 48
  Blow the Man Down...............................49
  Harem Dance..49
  Note Summary 50

● **LESSON 12**
  F Major Chord 51
  C Seventh Chord 51
  Turnaround Progressions 52
  Alternative Chord Fingerings 53

● **LESSON 13**
  Rests...54
  The Common Time Signature 54
  Banks of the Ohio.................................55

Contents Continued

LESSON 14

Sixth String Notes 56
I Gave My Love a Cherry 57
12 Bar Blues in the Key of C 57
Asturias 58
Open Position Notes 59

LESSON 15

Eighth Notes 60
Alternate Picking 60
12 Bar Blues in the Key of C 61
Waltzing Matilda 62
Duets 62
Song of Joy 63

LESSON 16

B Minor Chord 64
B Seventh Chord 65

LESSON 17

Sharps 66
House of the Rising Sun 67
Dark Eyes 67
Minuet 68

LESSON 18

Flats 69
8 Bar Blues 71
First and Second Endings 71
Hall of the Mountain King 72

LESSON 19

Silent Strums and Continuous Rhythm 73
Silent Strum Symbols 73
Rhythm Variations 74
Blues Traveller 75
Blue Seas 75

LESSON 20

Dotted Quarter Notes 76
Greensleeves 76
The 'High' A Note 77
Scarborough Fair 77
Auld Lang Syne 78

LESSON 21

Suspended Chords 79
Suspended Blues 81

LESSON 22

More on Bass Note Rhythm Patterns 82
Arkansas Traveller 84
Alternate Bass Note Picking 85
God Rest Ye Merry Gentlemen 86

LESSON 23

The Major Scale 87
The C Major Scale 87
The Key of C Major 87
Morning Has Broken 88

LESSON 24

The G Major Scale 89
Key Signatures 89
C Major Key Signature 89
G Major Key Signature 89
All Through the Night 90
Lavender's Blue 90

LESSON 25

The F Major Scale 91
F Major Key Signature 91
The Galway Piper 91
Mary Ann 92
Folk Dance 92

LESSON 26

The Eighth Rest 93
Syncopation 94
Elemental Syncopation Blues 94
Jamaica Farewell 95

APPENDIX ONE

Tuning 96

APPENDIX TWO

Chord Chart 99

APPENDIX THREE

Glossary of Musical Terms 100

Other Titles by Koala Music Publications

Koala Music Publications has a large variety of music instruction books including a whole series of Guitar Methods and comprehensive Guitar Manuals.

While you are studying this book, you will find *Progressive Guitar Method Book 1: Supplement* and *Progressive Guitar Method: Theory* particularly useful. On completion of this book, you will be ready to study specific types of guitar playing such as Rhythm, Lead, and Fingerpicking.

Shown below are some of the other titles published by Koala Music Publications.

Beginner Basics Guitar Bible

An indispensable self-teaching, learning and reference manual for the beginning Guitarist. Hardcover, Glossy Full Colour, 332-page manual with 90 lessons covering Lead, Rhythm and Fingerpicking styles. Contains 5DVDs, and DVD-rom with over 570 audio and 350 video files to download to PC, Mac, iPod or MP3 player.

Progressive Guitar for Adults

52 Full colour, step-by-step lessons to learn to play any style of guitar. Covers both melody and chord playing including both open position and moveable shapes along with all the essential techniques for both rhythm and lead guitar playing. Also covers understanding rhythms, scales and keys and how to write your own music. All examples sound great and are fun to play.

Progressive Guitar Method: Book 1: Supplement

A collection of over 70 well known songs with chord symbols which can be used along or in conjunction with Progressive Guitar Method Book 1. Contains 8 more lessons on major scales, keys, triplets, 6/8 time, 16th notes, syncopation and swing rhythms.

Progressive Guitar Method: Rhythm

Introduces all the important open chord shapes for major, minor, seventh, sixth, major seventh, minor seventh, suspended, diminished and augmented chords. Learn to play over 50 chord progressions, including 12 Bar Blues and Turnaround progressions.

Progressive Guitar Method: Lead

Covers scales and patterns over the entire fretboard so that you can improvise against major, minor, and Blues progressions in any key. Learn the licks and techniques used by all lead guitarists such as hammer-ons, slides, bending, vibrato, and more.

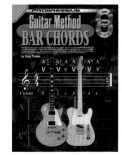

Progressive Guitar Method: Fingerpicking

Introduces right hand fingerpicking patterns that can be used as an accompaniment to any chord, chord progression or song. Covers alternate thumb, arpeggio and constant bass styles as used in Rock, Pop, Folk, Country, Blues Ragtime and Classical music.

Progressive Guitar Method: Chords

Contains the most useful open, Bar and Jazz chord shapes of the most used chord types with chord progressions to practice and play along with. Includes sections on tuning, how to read sheet music, transposing, as well as an easy chord table, formula and symbol chart.

Progressive Guitar Method: Bar Chords

Introduces the most useful Bar, Rock and Jazz chord shapes used by all Rock/Pop/Country and Blues guitarists. Includes major, minor, seventh, sixth, major seventh, etc. Suggested rhythm patterns including percussive strums, dampening and others are also covered.

Progressive Guitar Method: Book 2

A comprehensive, lesson by lesson method covering the most important keys and scales for guitar, with special emphasis on bass note picking, bass note runs, hammer-ons etc. Featuring chordal arrangements of well known Rock, Blues, Folk and Traditional songs.

Progressive Guitar Method: Theory Book 1

A comprehensive introduction to music theory as it applies to the guitar. Covers reading traditional music, rhythm notation and tablature, along with learning the notes on the fretboard, how to construct chords and scales, transposition, musical terms and playing in all keys.

Introduction

THE PROGRESSIVE GUITAR METHOD is a series of books designed to take the Guitar student from a beginner level through to a professional standard of playing. All books are carefully graded, lesson by lesson methods which assume no prior knowledge on your behalf. Within the series all styles and techniques of guitar playing are covered, including reading music, playing chords and rhythms, lead guitar and fingerpicking.

PROGRESSIVE GUITAR METHOD BOOK 1: NOTES, CHORDS AND RHYTHMS assumes you have no prior knowledge of music or playing the guitar. Starting with the different types of guitars available and the different styles of playing you are :

1.   Introduced to the notes on each of the six strings, together with basic elements of music theory including time signatures, note values, sharps, flats and the chromatic scale. This theory is essential to help you understand the guitar and can be applied to solve practical problems, hence speeding up your progress.
2.   Introduced to all the important open chord shapes for major, minor and seventh chords;
2.   Learn to play over many chord progressions, including 12 Bar Blues and Turnaround progressions.
3.   Learn to play rhythm patterns using easy read rhythm notation.

This book also has special sections on tuning, how to read sheet music and a chord chart.
All guitarists should know all of the information contained in these books. This book will provide you with a solid understanding of guitar chords and rhythms. In conjunction with this book you can use other books in the Progressive series to learn about lead guitar playing, fingerpicking, bar chords, slide and classical guitar styles as well as music theory and different styles such as Rock, Blues, Country, Jazz, Metal and Funk.

The best and fastest way to learn is to use these books in conjunction with:
1.   Buying sheet music and song books of your favourite recording artists and learning to play their songs.
2.   Practicing and playing with other musicians. You will be surprised how good a basic drums/bass/ guitar combination can sound even when playing easy music.
3.   Learning by listening to your favourite songs and albums.

Also in the early stages it is helpful to have the guidance of an experienced teacher. This will also help you keep to a schedule and obtain weekly goals.

Approach to Practice

It is important to have a correct approach to practice. You will benefit more from several short practices (e.g. 15-30 minutes per day) than one or two long sessions per week. This is especially so in the early stages, because of the basic nature of the material being studied. In a practice session you should divide your time evenly between the study of new material and the revision of past work. It is a common mistake for semi-advanced students to practice only the pieces they can already play well. Although this is more enjoyable, it is not a very satisfactory method of practice. You should also try to correct mistakes and experiment with new ideas. It is the authors' belief that an experienced teacher will be an invaluable aid to your progress.

Using the Accompanying DVDs, DVD-ROMs and CDs

The accompanying discs contain video and audio recordings of the examples in this book. An exercise number and a play icon on a colored strip indicates a recorded example:

 57 ⟵ **CD TRACK / DVD MENU NUMBER**

The book shows you where to put your fingers and what techniques to use, and the recordings let you hear and see how each example should sound and look when performed correctly.

DVD Angle Option 1

Practice the examples slowly at first on your own. Then try playing to a metronome set to a slow tempo, such that you can play the example evenly and without stopping. Gradually increase the tempo as you become more confident and then you can try playing along with the recording.

You will hear a drum beat at the beginning of each example, to lead you into the example and to help you keep time.

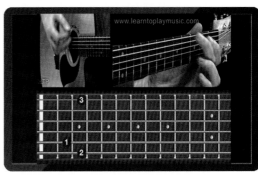

Your guitar must be in tune with the recordings to play along (see the "Tuning Your Guitar" section at the end of the book).

Included with this book:

DVD Angle Option 2

* **2 DVDs**, which can be played in any DVD player and contain all the exercises in this book with multiple camera angles, fretboard animations and full scrolling scores (displayed above). These are accessed from your DVD player remote using the video angle button available on most DVD players. Also, you can choose between several audio options including 'main part with backing track' (so you can hear how the guitar should sound with a band), 'solo main part' (so you can hear the guitar by itself) or 'backing track only' (so you can play along). These audio angles (or language tracks) are also accessed from the DVD remote.

* **1 DVD-ROM**, which can be used in any computer and most gaming consoles and portable media players (e.g. iPod, Xbox, Playstation etc) and contains all the audio and video for all exercises in this book. Both discs contain identical content but one is for use with Microsoft Windows Media Player (included free with all Windows PCs) and the other for Apple iTunes and Quicktime Media Player (included free with all Apple Mac computers and available for Windows PCs via free download at www.apple.com). On both discs you will find two folders, one containing the video examples and the other containing the audio examples. Follow the instructions for your media player to import these files to your hard drive and transfer to your portable media player if required.

* **1 CD**, which can be played in any CD player. Due to the limitations of the CD format not all examples are present on the CD.

Tips

* Most CD, DVD and portable media players have the ability to repeat tracks. You can make good use of this feature to practice the examples a number of times without stopping.

* The latest versions of both Windows Media Player and Quicktime Player (available with iTunes) have the ability to slow down the speed of the recorded exercises while still maintaining the correct pitch. This is very handy for practicing the more complex pieces.

Electronic Tuner

The easiest and most accurate way to tune your guitar is by using an **electronic tuner**. An electronic tuner allows you to tune each string individually to the tuner, by indicating whether the notes are sharp (too high) or flat (too low). If you have an electric guitar you can plug it directly into the tuner. If you have an acoustic guitar the tuner will have an inbuilt microphone. There

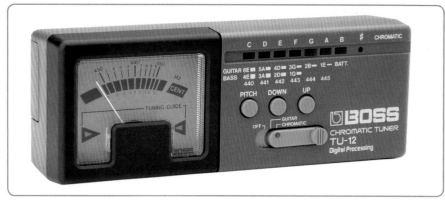

Electronic Tuner

are several types of electronic guitar tuners but most are relatively inexpensive and simple to operate. Tuning using other methods is difficult for beginning guitarists and it takes many months to master, so we recommend you purchase an electronic tuner, particularly if you do not have a guitar teacher or a friend who can tune it for you. Also if your guitar is way out of tune you can always take it to your local music store so they can tune it for you. Once a guitar has been tuned correctly it should only need minor adjustments before each practice session. To learn to tune the guitar using other methods see page 97.

Tuning Your Guitar to the Recording

Before you commence each lesson or practice session you will need to tune your guitar. If your guitar is out of tune everything you play will sound incorrect even though you are holding the correct notes. On the accompanying CD, the first track has a recording of each of the six strings of the guitar. These are also on the DVD and the DVD-ROM. For a complete description of how to tune your guitar, see page 97.

 1.0 6th String **E Note** (Thickest string)   **1.1** 5th String **A Note**   **1.2** 4th String **D Note**

 1.3 3rd String **G Note**   **1.4** 2nd String **B Note**   **1.5** 1st String **E Note** (Thinnest string)

Acoustic Guitars

Classical Guitar
(Nylon Strings)

Steel String Acoustic

The **classical guitar** has nylon strings and a wider neck than other types of guitar. It is most commonly used for playing Classical, Flamenco and Fingerstyles. Generally it is much cheaper than other types of guitar and is recommended for beginning guitarists.

The **steel string acoustic** has steel strings and is most commonly played by strumming or fingerpicking groups of notes called chords. This is the type of acoustic guitar you will hear in most modern styles of music e.g. Acoustic Rock, Pop, Folk, Country, Blues and World music.

Electric Guitars

Electric guitars have **pick-ups** (a type of inbuilt microphone) and need to be played into an **amplifier** (amp) to be heard.

The **solid body electric** is commonly used in Metal, Rock, Blues and Pop. Famous solid body guitars are the **Gibson Les Paul** and the **Fender Stratocaster**.

The **hollow body electric** (semi acoustic) is most commonly used in Jazz and Blues.

Acoustic guitars can be amplified by placing a microphone near the sound hole or by placing a portable pick-up on the body of the guitar. This is common for performances at large venues where the acoustic guitar needs amplification to be heard.

Electric Guitars *(PLAYED THROUGH AN AMPLIFIER)*

Solid Body Electric

Hollow Body Electric
(semi acoustic)

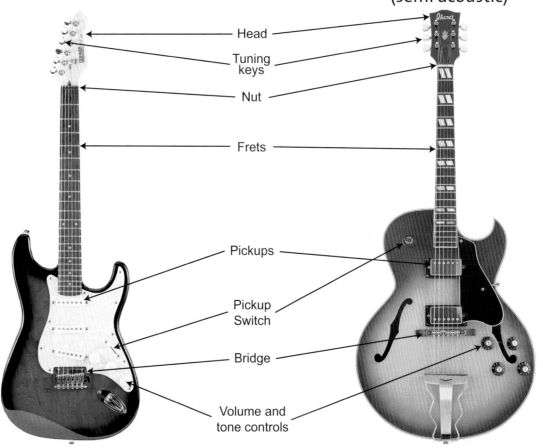

Head

Tuning keys

Nut

Frets

Pickups

Pickup Switch

Bridge

Volume and tone controls

Amplifiers

Combo
(combined amp and speaker)

Stack
(separate amp head and speaker)

Strings

It is important to have the correct set of strings fitted to your guitar, especially if you are a beginner. Until you build enough strength in your hands to fret the chords cleanly, light gauge or low tension strings are recommended. A reputable music store which sells guitar strings should be able to assist with this. Do not put steel strings on a classical guitar as they will damage the neck of the guitar. It is important to change your strings regularly, as old strings go out of tune easily and are more difficult to keep in tune.

Seating

Before you commence playing, a comfortable seating position is required. Most modern guitarists prefer to sit with their right leg raised, (as shown in the photo) or by placing their right foot on a footstool. The guitar should be close to the body, and in a vertical position. The main aim is for comfort and easy access to the guitar. A music stand will also be helpful.

Standing

1   Use a wide guitar strap and adjust it to a comfortable length. Let the strap take the weight of the guitar. This will keep your hands free to play rather than having to support the instrument.
2   Make sure your weight is balanced evenly between both feet.
3   The guitar should sit comfortably against your body in an upright position, with the neck pointing slightly upwards.

The standing position is particularly good for playing electric guitar and is essential if you plan to play in a band. Once you are comfortable with this position, try moving in time with the music as you play.

Right Hand and Arm
Using the Pick

The right hand is used to play the strings by plucking them with a pick.
A pick is a piece of plastic shaped like a triangle.

Hold the pick lightly between your thumb and first finger, as shown in the following photo.

Use the tip of the pick to play the string.

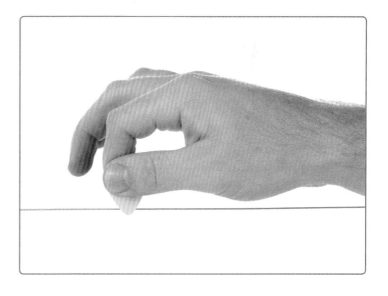

Right Arm Position

The correct position for the right arm is illustrated in **Photo A** below. Notice that the fore-arm rests on the upper edge of the guitar, just below the elbow. Be careful not to have the elbow hanging over the face of the guitar or your hand too far along the fretboard (**Photo B**).

Photo A: CORRECT

Photo B: INCORRECT

The Left Hand

The left hand fingers are numbered as such:

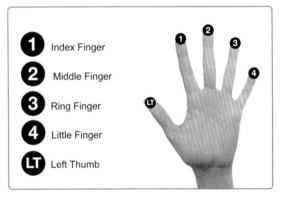

1 Index Finger
2 Middle Finger
3 Ring Finger
4 Little Finger
LT Left Thumb

Left Hand Placement

Your fingers should be **on their tips** and placed just **left** of the frets (not on top of them).

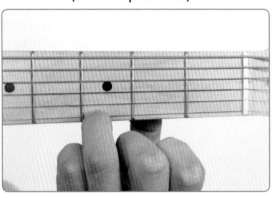

Be careful not to allow the thumb to hang too far over the top of the neck (**Photo C**), or to let it run parallel along the back of the neck (**Photo D**).

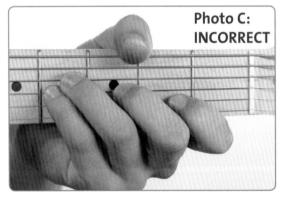

Photo C: INCORRECT

CORRECT

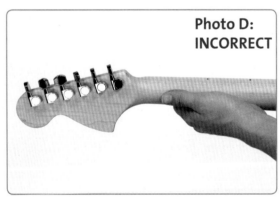

Photo D: INCORRECT

CORRECT

The Rudiments of Music

The musical alphabet consists of 7 letters:

A B C D E F G

Music is written on a **staff**, which consists of 5 parallel lines between which there are 4 spaces.

Music Staff

The treble or 'G' clef is placed at the beginning of each staff line. This clef indicates the position of the note G. (It is an old fashioned method of writing the letter G, with the centre of the clef being written on the second staff line.)

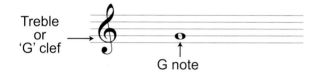

The other lines and spaces on the staff are named as such:

Extra notes can be added by the use of short lines, called **leger lines**.

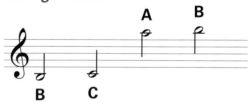

When a note is placed on the staff its head indicates its position, e.g.:

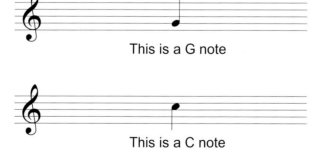

This is a G note

This is a C note

When the note head is below the middle staff line the stem points upward and when the head is above the middle line the stem points downward. A note placed on the middle line (**B**) can have its stem pointing either up or down.

Bar lines are drawn across the staff, which divides the music into sections called **bars** or **measures**. A **double bar line** signifies either the end of the music, or the end of an important section of it.

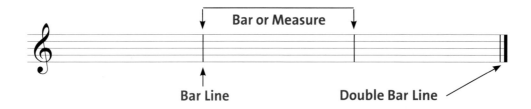

Note Values

The following table sets out the most common notes used in music and their respective time values (i.e. length of time held). For each note value there is an equivalent rest, which indicates a period of silence.

Whole Note and Rest (Semibreve)	Half Note and Rest (Minim)	Quarter Note and Rest (Crotchet)	Eighth Note and Rest (Quaver)	Sixteenth Note and Rest (Semiquaver)

4	2	1	1/2	1/4

If a **DOT** is placed after a note it increases the value of that note by half, e.g.

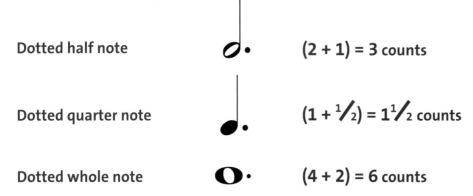

Dotted half note $(2 + 1) = 3$ counts

Dotted quarter note $(1 + \frac{1}{2}) = 1\frac{1}{2}$ counts

Dotted whole note $(4 + 2) = 6$ counts

A **tie** is a curved line joining two or more notes of the same pitch, where the second note(s) **is note played** but its time value is added to that of the first note. Here are two examples:

| 2 | + | 1 | = 3 counts | | 4 | + | 2 + 1 | = 7 counts |

In both of these examples only the first note is played.

Time Signatures

At the beginning of each piece of music, after the treble clef, is the **time signature**.

Time Signature
(pronounced Four Four time)

The time signature indicates the number of beats per bar (the top number) and the type of note receiving one beat (the bottom number). For example:

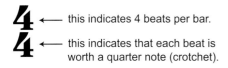

← this indicates 4 beats per bar.

← this indicates that each beat is
   worth a quarter note (crotchet).

Thus in $\frac{4}{4}$ time there must be the equivalent of 4 quarter note beats per bar, e.g.

$\frac{4}{4}$ is the most common time signature and is sometimes represented by this symbol called **common time**.

common time

The other time signature used in this book is Three Four Time written $\frac{3}{4}$.
$\frac{3}{4}$ indicates 3 quarter note beats per bar, e.g.

Count, Pick and Fingering Symbols

In the music throughout this book, you will notice symbols representing a metronome (⛯), a pick (♡) and a hand symbol (✋). The metronome symbol (as shown in the above piece) tells you what to count for the particular example. The pick shows you the pick motion and the hand represents left hand fingering.

Chord Diagrams

Chords are learnt with the help of a **chord diagram**. This will show you exactly where to place your left hand fingers in order to play a particular chord. A chord diagram is a grid of horizontal and vertical lines representing the strings and frets of the guitar as shown below.

Chord Symbol → **C**

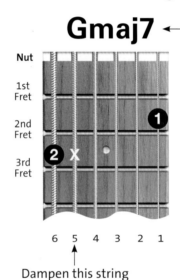

String Number

The 6th string is the thickest

The 1st string is the thinnest

Left Hand Fingering

1 Index Finger   **3** Ring Finger

2 Middle Finger   **4** Little Finger

The **coloured dots** show you where to place your left hand fingers. There are three basic types of chords- **major** (shown as red dots), **minor** (purple dots) and **dominant** (green dots). The **white number** tells you which finger to place on the string just before the fret. If there is no dot on a string, you play it as an open (not fretted) string. The other chord diagram symbols used in this book are summarized with the following two chord shapes.

Dm7 ← Chord symbol for D minor seventh chord.

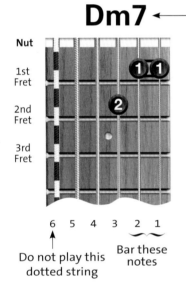

6 5 4 3 2 1

Do not play this dotted string

Bar these notes

A **dotted** string indicates that string is not to be strummed. A small **bar** connecting two black dots indicates they are held down by the same finger. This is called **barring**.

Gmaj7 ← Chord symbol for G major seventh chord.

6 5 4 3 2 1

Dampen this string with the **second finger** by lightly touching it.

An **X** on the string indicates that string is to **dampened** by another finger lightly touching it. The string is still strummed as a part of the chord but it is not heard.

Rhythm Symbols

1   2

This is a **half note strum**. It lasts for **two** beats. There are **two** half note strums in one bar of $\frac{4}{4}$ time.

1   +

These are a pair of **eighth note strums**. Each strum lasts for **half a beat**. There are **eight** eighth note strums in one bar of $\frac{4}{4}$ time. Play the larger downward strum louder.

1   +   a

This is a group of three **eighth note triplet strums**. Each strum in the group lasts for **one third** of a beat. There are **twelve** eighth note triplet strums in one bar of $\frac{4}{4}$ time. Play the larger downward strum louder.

V

1

This is a **quarter note strum**. It lasts for **one** beat. There are **four** quarter note strums in one bar of $\frac{4}{4}$ time.

1   e   +   a

These Strums are a group of **sixteenth note strums**. Each strum lasts for **one quarter** of a beat. There are **sixteen** sixteenth note strums in one bar of $\frac{4}{4}$ time. Play the larger downward strum louder.

1

A broken strum symbol indicates that the strings are not to be strummed.

LESSON ONE

First String Notes

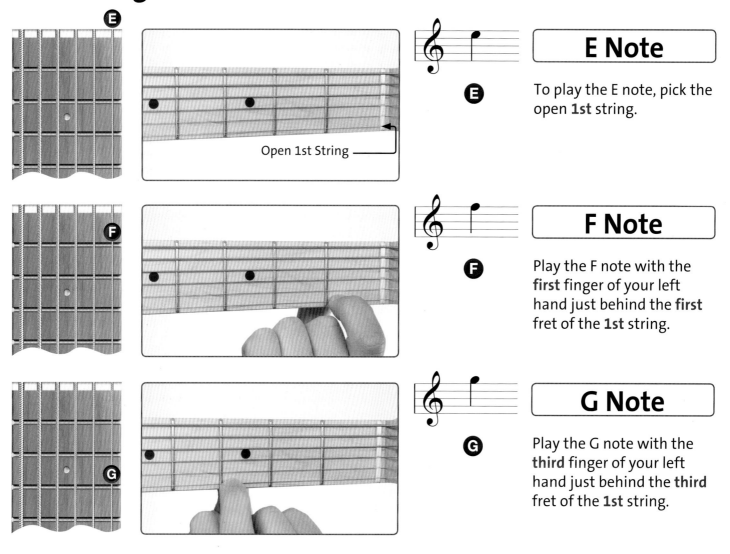

E Note

To play the E note, pick the open **1st** string.

F Note

Play the F note with the **first** finger of your left hand just behind the **first** fret of the **1st** string.

G Note

Play the G note with the **third** finger of your left hand just behind the **third** fret of the **1st** string.

Place your fingers **on their tips**, immediately **behind** the frets and **press** hard to avoid buzzing or deadened notes.

The following examples use **quarter notes** (or crotchets) ♩, worth one count each **(see page 16)**.

Use a **downward** pick motion V. This will apply to all examples and songs until otherwise instructed.

▶ 2.0

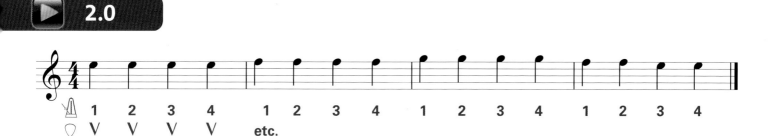

1   2   3   4   etc.

1   2   3   4   etc.

Right Hand Support

It is necessary for the right hand to be supported on the guitar by either (**1**) the palm resting against the bridge or (**2**) resting fingers on the pick guard. This will feel more comfortable and aid in the development of speed by encouraging a down/up movement rather than an in/out movement of the pick.

(1) Palm support on bridge

(2) Finger support on pick guard

Pick Technique

You should not let the pick 'dig in' to the strings, but rather play using only its tip.

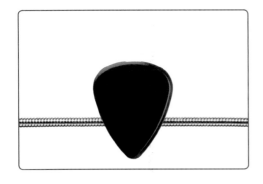

INCORRECT

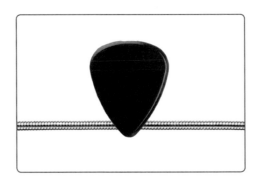

CORRECT

Trouble shooting

•Play **slowly** and **evenly. Do not** attempt to go fast as accuracy is more important at this level.
•Place your fingers directly **behind** the frets (**as shown in the photos**) and **on their tips.**
•**Count** (in groups of four) in your head or out loud as you play.
•Be sure to support your wrist and use correct pick technique.

LESSON TWO

Second String Notes

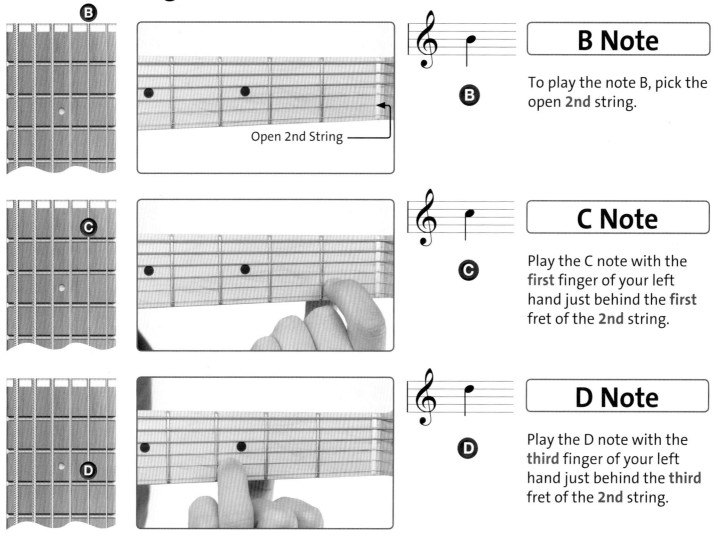

B Note

To play the note B, pick the open **2nd** string.

C Note

Play the C note with the **first** finger of your left hand just behind the **first** fret of the **2nd** string.

D Note

Play the D note with the **third** finger of your left hand just behind the **third** fret of the **2nd** string.

Ex. 3.0 introduces the **half note** (or minim) ♩, which is worth two counts. In bar 8 the half notes are played on the first and third beats, as indicated by the count. This exercise is 8 bars long. Also note the small bar numbers written below the staff.

▶ 3.0

Troubleshooting

- Make sure your guitar is in tune (**see Appendix One, page 97**).
- **Watch the music**, not your fingers.
- Concentrate on learning the notes, rather than memorising the song. To do this, you should play very slowly, naming each note as you play it.
- Remember to use the correct fingering: **first** finger for **first** fret notes, and **third** finger for **third** fret notes.

The following songs make use of all six notes that you have learned so far.

3.1   Song of Joy (Part One)

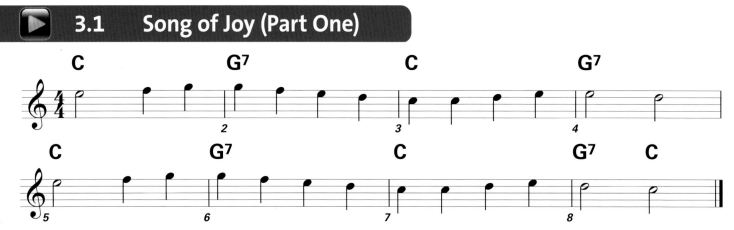

* **Chord symbols** have been included for students who have some chord knowledge.
You will learn about chords in the following lesson. Chord symbols indicate the chords to be played as an accompaniment to the melody.

3.2   Skip to My Lou

3.3   Steps and Skips

LESSON THREE

Before commencing each lesson or practice session, make sure that your guitar is in tune.
See page 97

The C Major Chord

A **chord** is a group of three or more notes that are played together. Chords are used to accompany a singer or an instrumentalist who is playing the melody of a song. The first chord you will learn is the **C major chord**, usually just called the **C chord**. Major chords are the most common chords. The C major chord is indicated by the letter **C**. Chords are written on chord diagrams as discussed in the introduction (page 18).

C

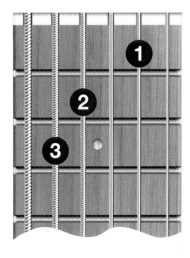

C Major Chord

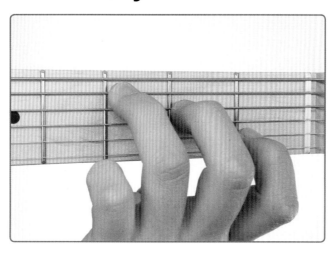

C

To play the **C** chord, place the **first** finger of your left hand just behind the **first** fret of the **second** string, the **second** finger just behind the **second** fret of the **fourth** string and your **third** finger just behind the **third** fret of the **fifth** string.

To play the C chord, play **all six** strings with the pick at the same time using a **downward** motion. This is called a **strum.** Hold the pick lightly and strum from the wrist. Keep your wrist relaxed. If any notes buzz or sound deadened you may have to press harder with the left hand fingers and make sure that your fingers are just behind the fret (not too far back).

Strumming

This is the symbol for a downward strum. This is a **quarter note strum**. It lasts for **one beat**. There are **four** quarter note strums in one bar of $\frac{4}{4}$ time.

This is a **whole note strum**. It lasts for **four beats**. There is **one** whole note strum in one bar of $\frac{4}{4}$ time.

In the following example there are four bars of the **C major** chord played in $\frac{4}{4}$ time. The chord symbol is written above the staff and a new chord symbol is placed at the beginning of each bar. Play the chord with four quarter note strums in each bar. To make the example sound finished always end with one strum of the first chord (a whole note strum ▽).

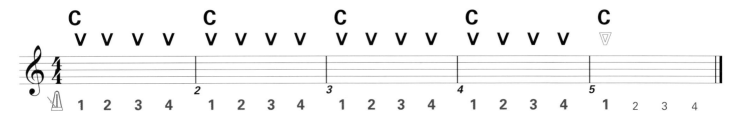

To help keep time play the first quarter note strum in each bar louder.

The Seventh Chord

Another type of common chord is called the **dominant seventh** chord. It is usually referred to as the "**seventh**" chord. The chord symbol for the seventh chord is the number **7** written after the alphabetical letter. The symbol for the **D seventh** chord is **D7**.

D7

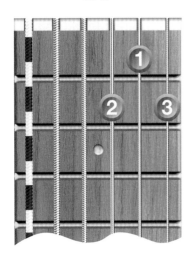

D Seventh Chord

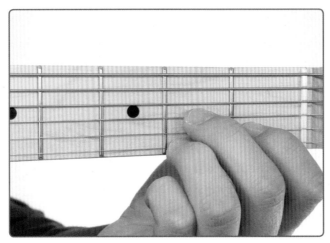

D7

To play the **D7** chord, use the first **three** fingers of your left hand as shown in the diagram, but strum only **five** strings. Do not strum the **6th** string (as indicated by the dotted line).

The Half Note Strum

This is a **half note strum**.

It lasts for **two** beats.

There are **two** half note strums in one bar of $\frac{4}{4}$ time.

In the example below there are four bars of the **D7** chord. Play the **D7** chord with two half note strums in each bar. The **bold** numbers tell you to strum the chord, the **smaller** numbers indicate to hold it until the next strum.

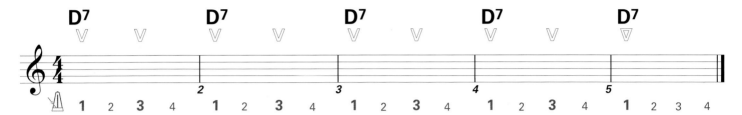

Chord Progressions

Now try using both the **C** and **D7** chords. This is a **chord progression.**

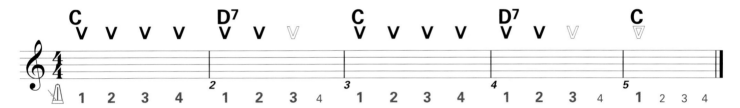

Pivot Finger

When changing between the **C** and **D7** chords, do not move your first finger, as it is common to both chords. The first finger acts as a **pivot** around which the other fingers move. This will make the chord changes easier. Practice slowly and evenly and count or tap your foot as you play to help you keep time.

There are four beats in each bar. When strumming, only your wrist should move. Do not move your arm and keep your forearm resting on the upper edge of the guitar. Remember to keep your left hand fingers just behind the fret. If you place it on top of the fret, the note will sound deadened. If you place it too far back from the fret, the note will buzz and you will have to press down harder to prevent it. If you have an acoustic guitar, pick the string over the sound hole as this results in the best sound.

G7

G Seventh Chord

G7

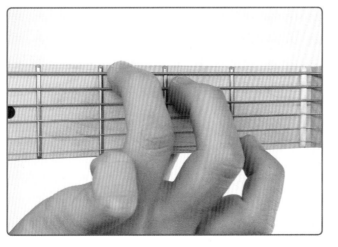

To play the **G7** chord, place the **first, second** and **third** fingers of your left hand as shown in the diagram. Strum all **six** strings.

The following chord progression contains all three chords you have learnt so far. Use the pivot finger when changing between C and D7.

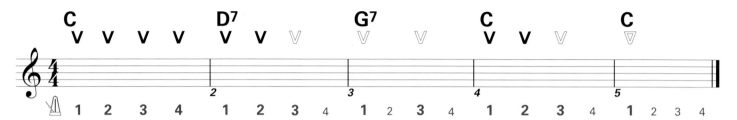

This chord progression contains two chords in each bar. Each chord receives two beats.

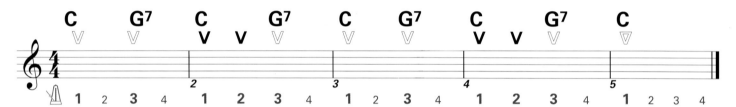

Rhythm Patterns

Instead of changing the strumming for each bar it is quite common to play the same pattern of strums throughout a chord progression. This is called a **rhythm pattern**. It is placed above the staff and indicates the strumming pattern to be played in each bar of music. Unless indicated otherwise, always end with one strum of the first chord (a whole note strum ▽).

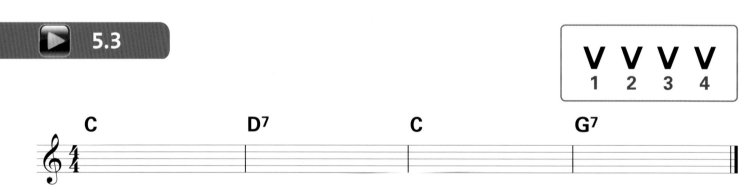

Open Chord Shapes

The chord shapes given in this lesson and throughout the remainder of the book are called **open chords** because they contain open strings (i.e. no finger is placed on the fret). Another type of chord to learn is called a bar chord. These are commonly used in Rock and Pop music. To learn about bar chords see *Progressive Guitar Method: Bar Chords*.

LESSON FOUR

12 Bar Blues

12 Bar Blues is a pattern of chords which repeats every 12 bars. There are hundreds of well known songs based on this chord progression, i.e. they contain basically the same chords in the same order.
12 bar Blues is common in many styles of music including Blues, Rock, Jazz, Country, Soul and Funk.
Some well known songs which use this 12 bar chord pattern are:

Original Batman TV Theme	Barbara Ann - The Beach Boys
Hound Dog - Elvis Presley	Johnny B Goode - Chuck Berry
Rock Around the Clock - Bill Haley	Dizzy Miss Lizzy - The Beatles
Roll Over Beethoven - Chuck Berry	Red House - Jimi Hendrix
Blue Suede Shoes - Elvis Presley	The Jack - ACDC
In the Mood - Glenn Miller	Ice Cream Man - Van Halen

 6   **12 Bar Blues in the Key of G**

The following 12 bar Blues is in the **key of G major** and uses all of the chords you have learnt so far.

This pattern of chords will probably sound familiar to you.
Instead of writing a chord symbol above each bar of music, it is common to write a symbol only when the chord changes e.g. the first four bars of this Blues are all **G7** chords. Once you can play this 12 bar Blues, use the chords to accompany **2 String Blues** on the following page.

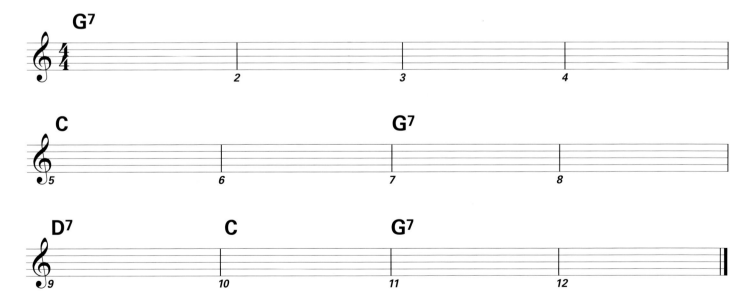

The Whole Note

This is a **whole note**.
It lasts for **four** beats.
There is **one** whole note in one bar of $\frac{4}{4}$ time.

2 String Blues introduces the **whole note (or semibreve)** in bar 12. It is worth four counts.
It is played on the first beat, and held for the remaining three, as indicated by the count.

7   2 String Blues

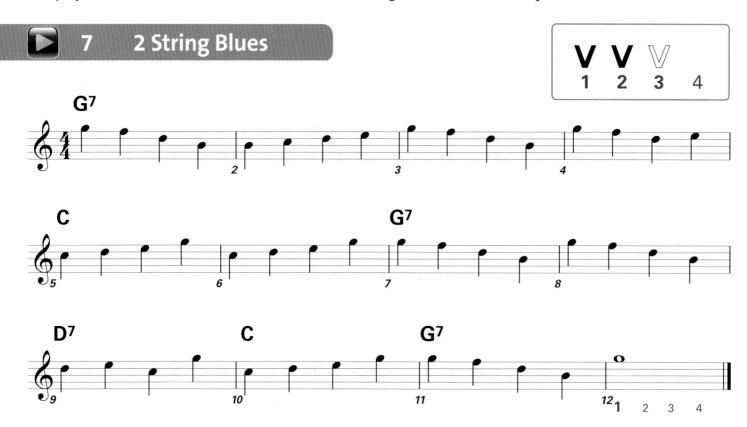

Know Your Guitars…
Larrivee Parlor Guitar

The Larrivee Parlor Guitar has a smaller body and shorter neck than standard acoustic guitars. This means the frets are closer together, making it easier for people with smaller hands to play . Despite its size, this guitar is surprisingly loud and has a beautiful tone. It's particularly good for Folk, Ragtime and Country Blues. Because of its smaller size, the Larrivee parlor guitar was chosen as the staff guitar on the International Space Station.

LESSON FIVE

Third String Notes

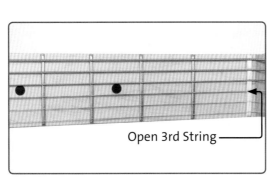

Open 3rd String

G Note

To play the note **G**, pick the open **3rd** string (no fingers placed behind the frets).

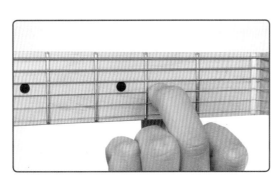

A Note

To play the note **A**, place the **second** finger of your left hand just behind the **second** fret of the **3rd** string.

▶ 8.0

The Octave

You now have two **G** notes; the one shown above and the one at the third fret on the first string. This type of repetition occurs with all notes, since the musical alphabet goes from **A** to **G**, and then back to **A** again. The distance between the two **G** notes is called an **octave**.

▶ 8.1

V	V	V	V
1	2	3	4

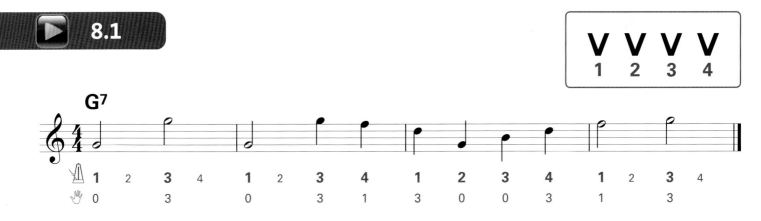

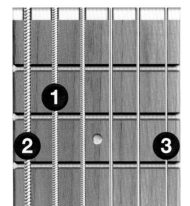

G

G Major Chord

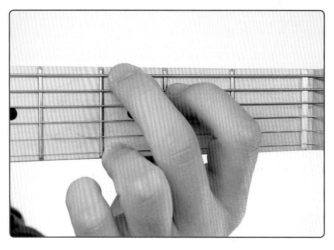

To play the **G** chord, place the **first**, **second** and **third** fingers of your left hand as shown in the diagram. Strum all **six** strings.

Slide Finger

 9.0 Changing from G to D7

The following example contains the **G** and **D7** chords.
When changing from **G** to **D7**, do not lift your third finger off the string, but slide it down to the second fret. Only touch the string very lightly as you do this.
When changing from **D7** to **G**, slide your third finger up to the third fret.

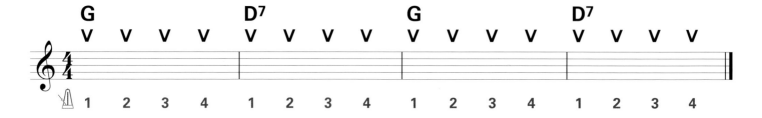

Here are some songs to practice your chord changes with.
These melodies contain all the notes you have learnt so far.

 9.1 Cycling in G

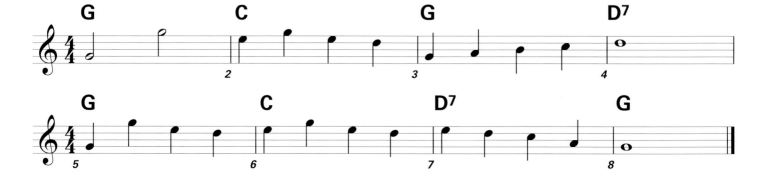

9.2   Three String Blues

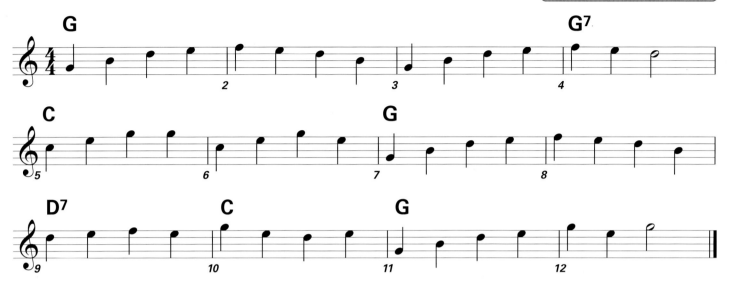

9.3   Guitar Boogie

Accessories…
Acoustic Guitar Pickups

Fingerpicking is mostly played on acoustic guitars. If you are playing in public, at some point you will need to amplify your guitar.
The most common way of doing this is to get a pickup fitted to your guitar and plug it into either an acoustic guitar amp, or the PA system used by the singer. There are many pickups available for acoustic guitars and most can be attached for a performance and then removed until required again.

LESSON SIX

Eighth Note Rhythms

All the rhythm patterns you have played so far involved playing a downward strum (**V**) on the 1st, 2nd, 3rd or 4th beat. To make rhythm patterns more interesting, **eighth note rhythm** patterns can be used. An eighth note rhythm is a combination of a down and an up strum within one beat. The down strum "on the beat" is played louder than the up strum which is "off the beat" (the "**+**" section of the count). An **up strum** is indicated by a **Λ**, and is played on the "**and**" section of the count. Start the up strum on the first (thinnest) string and strum all six strings.

Play the following rhythm pattern, which has eighth note strums on the second beat consisting of a down strum on the "2" count and an up strum on the "+" section of the count. There are **eight** eighth note strums in one bar of $\frac{4}{4}$ time.

 10   **Eighth Note Rhythm Pattern 1**

Practice this new rhythm pattern holding a **G** chord then apply it to the chord progression below.

```
V  VΛV  V
1  2 + 3  4
```

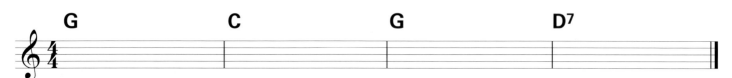

G   C   G   D⁷

 **11.0-11.7**

11.0
```
VΛV  V  V
1 + 2  3  4
```

11.1
```
V  V  V  VΛ
1  2  3  4 +
```

11.2
```
V  V  VΛV
1  2  3 + 4
```

11.3
```
VΛVΛVΛVΛ
1 + 2 + 3 + 4 +
```

11.4
```
VΛVΛV  V
1 + 2 + 3  4
```

11.5
```
V  VΛV  VΛ
1  2 + 3  4 +
```

11.6
```
VΛVΛVΛV
1 + 2 + 3 + 4
```

11.7
```
V  VΛVΛV
1  2 + 3 + 4
```

12.0   12 Bar Blues

V V∧V∧V
1 2 + 3 + 4

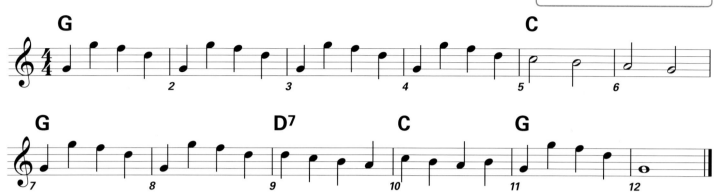

The Lead-In

This song introduces **lead-in notes**, which are notes occurring before the first complete bar of music. These notes should be played on counts three and four of a count-in (as indicated). You will notice that the final bar of the song contains only one half note (two counts), which acts as a 'balance' to the lead-in notes. This is quite common, but does not always occur. Lead-in notes are sometimes called pick up notes.

 12.1   **Michael Row the Boat Ashore**

V V∧V V∧
1 2 + 3 4 +

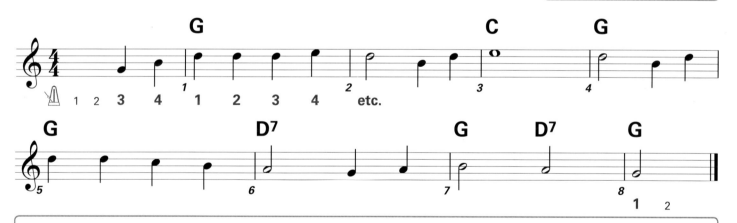

Classic Amps…
The Marshall Stack

The most famous Rock guitar amp of them all, the Marshall 100 watt amp with a 4x12 inch speaker "Quad box" has been widely used since it was invented by Jim Marshall in the 1960's. The term "stack" means an amp sitting on top of a separate speaker box. Marshall amps produce great overdriven sounds which are perfect for both Rhythm and Lead Rock guitar.

LESSON SEVEN

A Major Chord

A

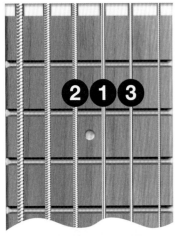

②①③

 13.0

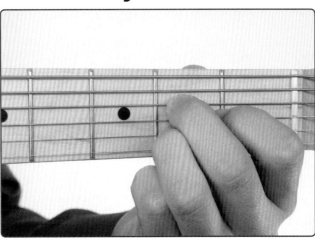

A

To play the **A** chord, place the **first, second** and **third** fingers of your left hand as shown in the diagram. Strum all **six** strings.

V	V	V	
1	**2**	**3**	4

When changing between **C** and **A** use your second finger as a pivot.

C	A	D⁷	G⁷

$\begin{array}{c} \\ \end{array}$ C | A | D^7 | G^7

E Major Chord

E

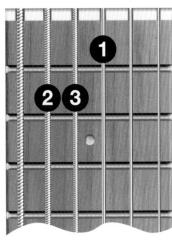

①

②③

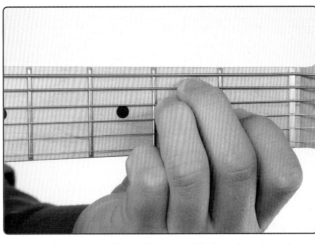

E

To play the **E** chord, place the **first, second** and **third** fingers of your left hand as shown in the diagram. Strum all **six** strings.

When changing from **E** to **A**, do not lift your first finger off the third string, but slide it down to the second fret. Only touch the third string very lightly as you do this. The use of the slide will make changing between **E** and **A** chords easier. Then play the following chord progression using the two bar rhythm pattern as shown.

 13.1

V	V	V	V	V	V	V	
1	**2**	**3**	**4**	**1**	**2**	**3**	4
First Bar				Second Bar			

E	A	E	A

The following chord progression uses the same two bar rhythm pattern as in the previous example, but contains two chords, each receiving two beats, in bars 1, 2 and 3.

13.2

E   A   E   C   E   A   C

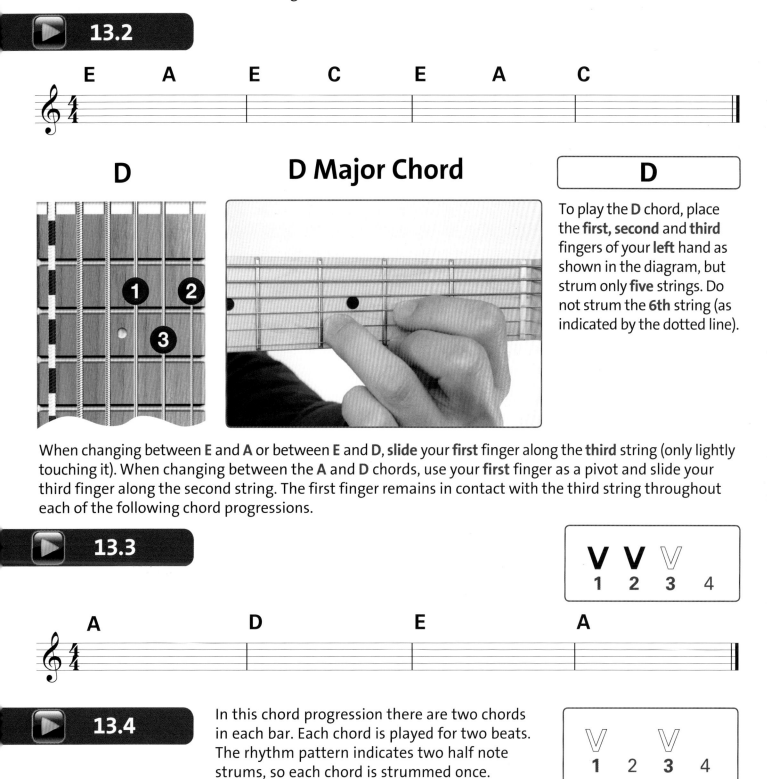

D Major Chord

D

To play the **D** chord, place the **first, second** and **third** fingers of your **left** hand as shown in the diagram, but strum only **five** strings. Do not strum the **6th** string (as indicated by the dotted line).

When changing between **E** and **A** or between **E** and **D**, **slide** your **first** finger along the **third** string (only lightly touching it). When changing between the **A** and **D** chords, use your **first** finger as a pivot and slide your third finger along the second string. The first finger remains in contact with the third string throughout each of the following chord progressions.

13.3

V V V
1 2 3 4

A   D   E   A

13.4

In this chord progression there are two chords in each bar. Each chord is played for two beats. The rhythm pattern indicates two half note strums, so each chord is strummed once. This progression is two bars long.
The two dots at the end of the progression is a repeat sign, which tells you to play the piece again from the beginning.

V V
1 2 3 4

E   A   D   A   Repeat Sign

LESSON EIGHT

12 Bar Blues and Seventh Chords

12 bar blues (and most chord progressions) can be played in any key. The following 12 bar Blues is in the **key of A major**. When a song is said to be in the key of **A major**, it means that the most important chord (and usually the first chord) is the **A** chord.

14   12 Bar Blues in the Key of A Major

V	V ∧ V ∧ V
1	2 + 3 + 4

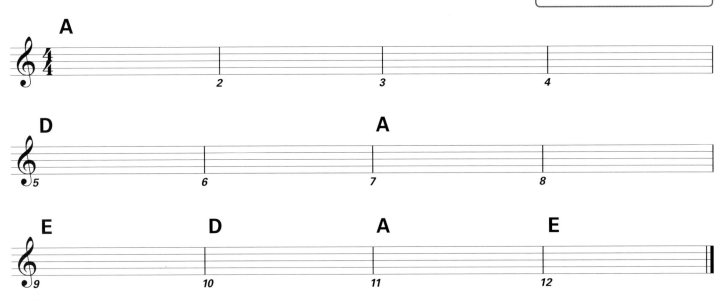

E Seventh Chord

E7

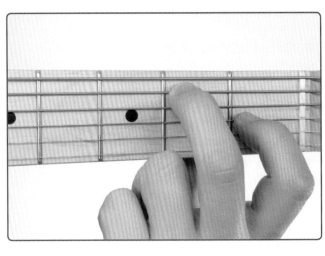

E7

To play the **E7** chord, use the **first** and **second** fingers of your left hand as shown in the diagram, and strum all **six** strings. The **E7** chord shape is just the **E** chord shape with the **third** finger lifted off.

15.0

The next chord progression contains an **E7** chord and uses the eighth note rhythm pattern shown on the right(introduced in exercise 10 on page 33). When changing between **D** and **E7** use your **first** finger as a **slide** finger. When changing between **A** and **D** use your **first** finger as a **pivot**.

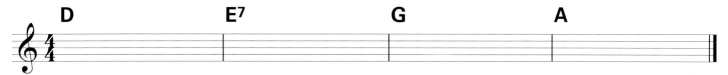

A7

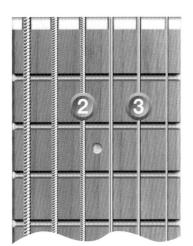

A Seventh Chord

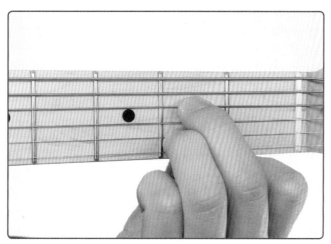

A7

To play the **A7** chord, use the **second** and **third** fingers of your left hand as shown in the diagram, and strum all **six** strings. The **A7** chord shape is just an **A** chord shape with the **first** finger lifted off.

15.1

This progression contains an **A7** chord and uses the eighth note rhythm pattern shown on the right (introduced in exercise 11.1 on page 33). When changing between **D7** and **G** use your **third** finger as a slide finger.

Know your Guitars...
Martin Dreadnought

In the early part of the 20th century, guitar manufacturer C.F. Martin released an acoustic guitar with a larger, deeper body than most existing guitars. Around the same time, the British navy launched a battleship that was so big it would fear nothing. It was called "HMS Dreadnought". Martin thought this would be a good name for his new guitar. The guitar sounded great and the name caught on. Today, the dreadnought is the most commonly used type of acoustic guitar in the world.

16.0 Bluesy Suzie

Here is a 12 bar Blues melody to be accompanied by the new chords you have learnt.

16.1 Aura Lee

A **repeat sign** in the final bar indicates that the song must be played again from the beginning. Repeat signs can also be used at the end of a section.
In this song the repeat sign at the end of bar 4 indicates a repeat of the first four bars.

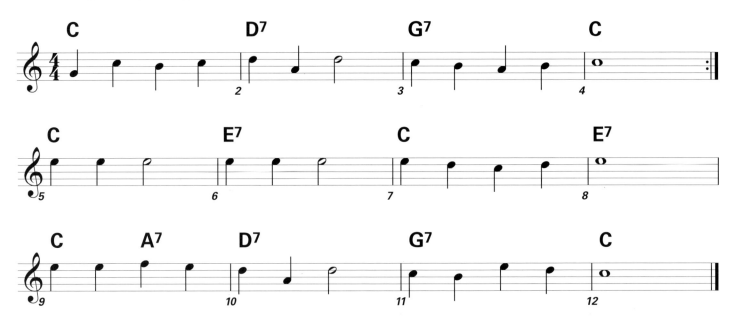

Note Summary

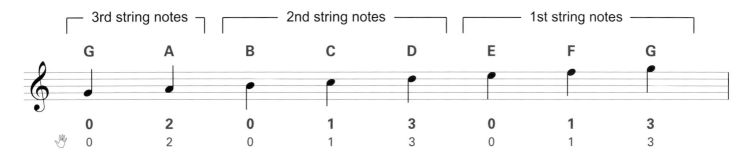

	3rd string notes		2nd string notes			1st string notes		
	G	A	B	C	D	E	F	G
	0	2	0	1	3	0	1	3
	0	2	0	1	3	0	1	3

Guitar Effects...
Loop Pedal

A great tool for both acoustic and electric guitar is the Loop pedal, which is basically a mini recording machine controlled by your foot. Plugging your guitar into a loop pedal enables you to play a chord progression and then get the pedal to loop it (repeat it) while you play another part or improvise over what you have just recorded.

Guitar Effects...
Chorus Pedal

The chorus pedal is an ambient effect which creates a feeling of space and movement within the sound. The pedal delays the sound and changes it to become less regular and also adds slight pitch fluctuations. It then mixes this version of the sound in with the original signal coming from the guitar. Chorus pedals are equally effective with both acoustic and electric guitars.

LESSON NINE

Minor Chords

There are three main types of chords: **Major**, **Seventh** and **Minor**. The chord symbol for the **minor** chord is a small '**m**' placed after the letter name. Here are some commonly used open minor chord shapes.

Dm

D Minor Chord

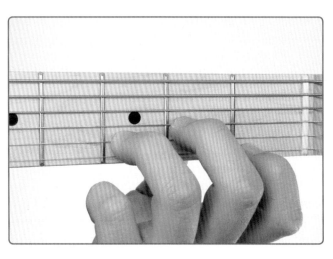

Dm

To play the **Dm** chord, use the **first**, **second** and **third** fingers of your left hand as shown in the diagram. Strum only **five** strings.

 ▶ **17.0**

In this progression use a **pivot** finger when changing from **C** to **A7** and **Dm** to **G7**. Use a **slide** finger between **A7** and **Dm**.

V	V ∧ V ∧ V
1	2 + 3 + 4

C	A⁷	Dm	G⁷

Am

A Minor Chord

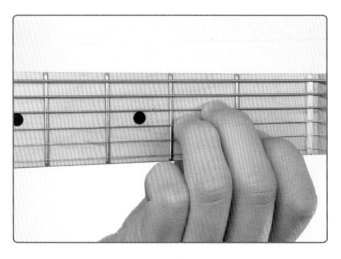

Am

To play the **Am** chord, use the **first**, **second** and **third** fingers of your left hand as shown in the diagram. Strum all **six** strings.

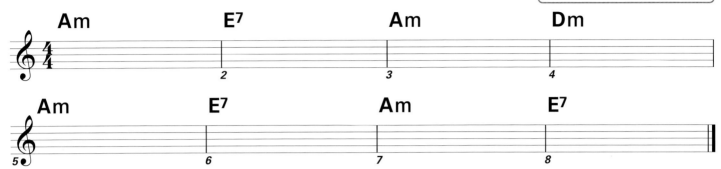

The Three Four Time Signature

This is the **three four time signature**. It indicates that there are **three** beats in each bar. Three four time is also known as waltz time. There are three quarter notes in one bar of $\frac{3}{4}$ time.

The following chord progression is written in $\frac{3}{4}$ time. To help keep time, accent (play louder) the first strum in each bar. Use your **first** and **second** fingers as **pivots** when changing between **C** and **Am**. Use your **first** finger as a **pivot** when changing between **Dm** and **G7**.

18.0

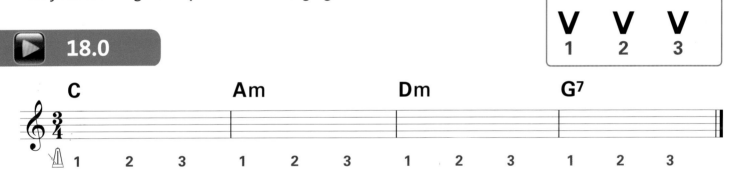

$\frac{3}{4}$ Time rhythm patterns

Practice the following $\frac{3}{4}$ time rhythm patterns holding a **C** chord shape. Apply any of these patterns to the above chord progression.

18.1-18.6

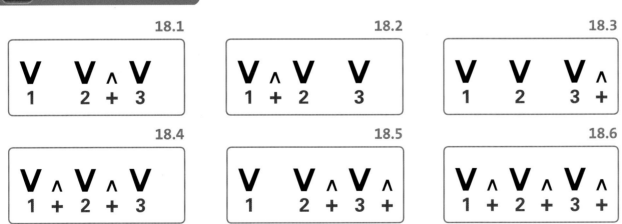

Em

E Minor Chord

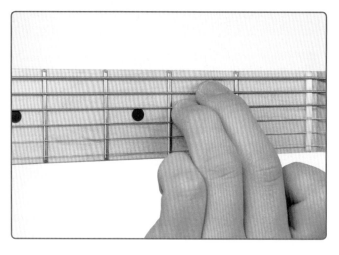

To play the **Em** chord, use the **second** and **third** fingers of your left hand as shown in the diagram. Strum all **six** strings. The **Em** chord shape is just the **E** chord shape with the **first** finger lifted off.

The following chord progression is in $\frac{3}{4}$ time and uses the three minor chords introduced. Use your **first** finger as a **pivot** when changing between **Dm** and **G7**. Use your **second** finger as a **pivot** when changing between **G7** and **Em**.

 18.7

V	V ∧ V	V	V	V
1	2 + 3	1	2	3

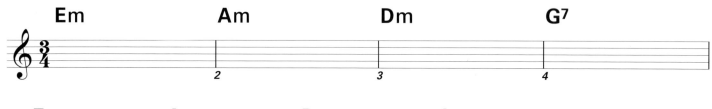

Em   Am   Dm   G7

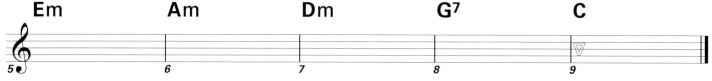

Em   Am   Dm   G7   C

Guitar Effects…
Wah Wah Pedal

The Wah Wah pedal imitates the "Wah" sound used by Jazz trumpeters waving a mute in front of the trumpet. It is a great expression tool for the electric guitar, enabling the guitarist to create talking and crying sounds by moving the foot up and down on the pedal. The Wah Wah pedal was made famous by Jimi Hendrix. He used a model called the "Cry Baby" which is shown in the accompanying photo.

Bass Note Rhythm Pattern

Bass notes are the notes on the 6th, 5th and 4th strings. Instead of strumming the complete chord for every beat, try picking the bass note of the chord on the first beat and then strum the first three or four strings of the chord on the 2nd and 3rd beats. Play the following bass note rhythm holding a **G** chord shape.

19.0

The best bass note to pick is the lowest note of the chord that has the same letter name of the chord. This is called the root note.

When playing a **G** chord, pick the 6th string note (**G** note).
When playing an **Em** chord, pick the 6th string note (**E** note).
When playing an **Am** chord, pick the 5th string note (**A** note).
When playing a **D7** chord, pick the 4th string note (**D** note).

Practice this rhythm technique on each chord separately at first, and remember to hold the full chord shape even though you are not playing all the strings.

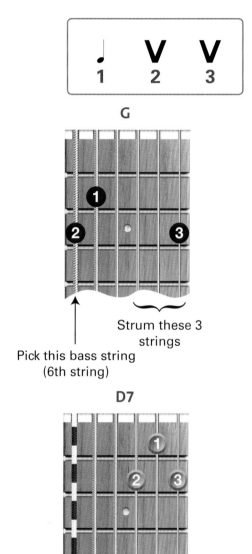

G

Strum these 3 strings

Pick this bass string (6th string)

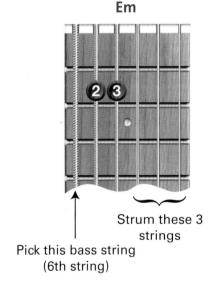

Em

Strum these 3 strings

Pick this bass string (6th string)

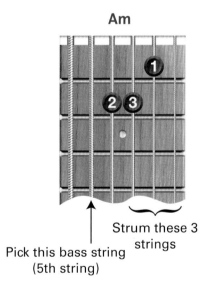

Am

Strum these 3 strings

Pick this bass string (5th string)

D7

Strum these 3 strings

Pick this bass string (4th string)

19.1

Play this chord progression using the bass note rhythm pattern.

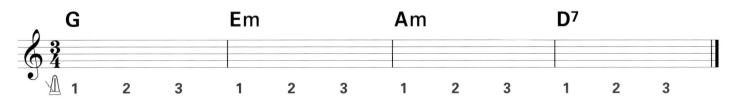

G   Em   Am   D⁷

1   2   3   1   2   3   1   2   3   1   2   3

LESSON TEN

Fourth String Notes

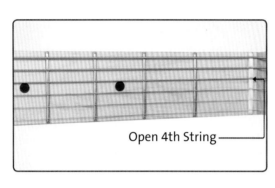

Open 4th String

D Note

To play the **D** note, pick the open **4th** string.

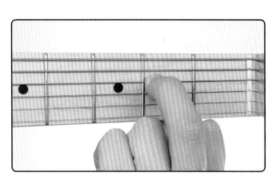

E Note

Play the **E** note with the **second** finger of your left hand behind the **second** fret of the **4th** string.

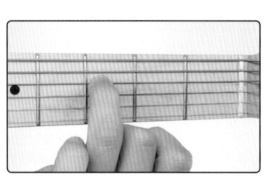

F Note

Play the **F** note with the **third** finger of your left hand behind the **third** fret of the **4th** string.

The Dotted Half Note

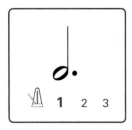

A dot placed after a note or strum extends its value by **half**. A dot placed after a half note or half note strum means that you hold it for three beats. One dotted half note makes one bar of music in ¾ time. There is one dotted half note strum in one bar of music in ¾ time. Use a dotted half strum to play the chords which accompany the following melody.

The Dotted Half Strum

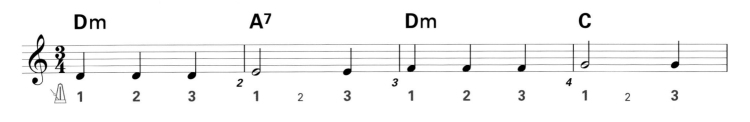

20.1   **Molly Malone**

Use the bass note rhythm pattern shown above to accompany this song.
Play the first **G** bass note where the **G** chord symbol is written above the first bar, rather than where the lead-in note occurs. Once you can play both the melody and accompaniment to a song, try playing one part while your teacher or another guitarist plays the other part. Then you can swap parts when the song repeats. This will prepare you for playing both rhythm and lead guitar.

The Tie

A **tie** is a curved line joining two or more notes of the same pitch. The second note (or notes) is **not played**, but its time value is added to that of the first note. In bar 1 the **G** note is held for a total of 4 counts (2+2) and in bar 15 it is held for 6 counts (4+2).

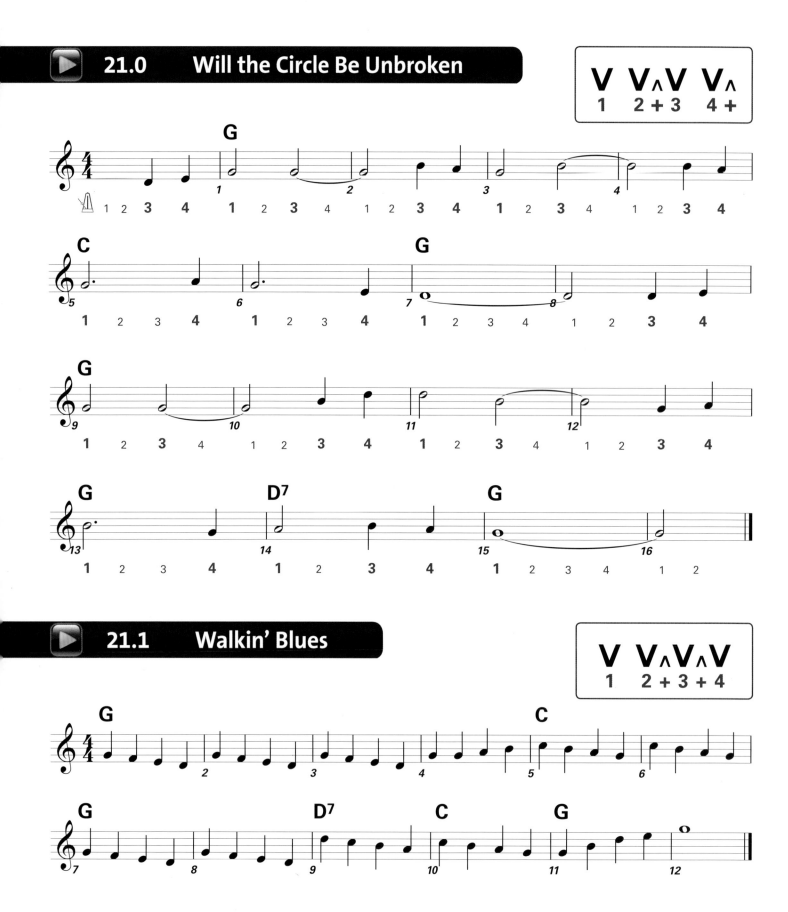

Note Summary

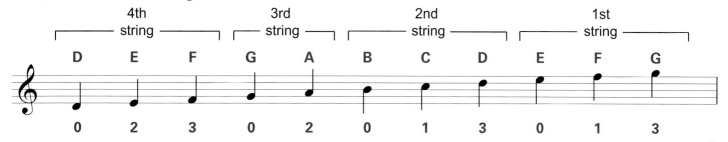

	4th string			3rd string			2nd string			1st string	
D	E	F	G	A	B	C	D	E	F	G
0	2	3	0	2	0	1	3	0	1	3

Troubleshooting

- Remember to maintain correct left and right hand playing positions (**see photos on page 14**).
- **Count** out loud as you play, and be particularly careful of dotted notes and ties. It may also help to tap your foot with the beat.
- Hold the pick correctly, between the thumb and index finger (**see page 13**).
- Be sure to support your wrist and use correct pick technique (**see page 20**).

Know your Guitars…
Rickenbacker 12 String

The electric guitar was invented by Adolf Rickenbacker in the 1930's. Rickenbacker guitars are now commonly used in Rock and Pop music. The Rickenbacker 12 string was made famous by George Harrison of the Beatles. It is also used by Roger McGuinn of the Byrds and by Tom Petty. 12 string guitars contain six courses of two strings side by side, with the two strings tuned an octave apart. The 12 string has a singing quality and is great for both chords and picking melodies.

Know your Guitars…
The Classical Guitar

The classical guitar has nylon strings and is played with the fingers of the right hand rather than a pick. As the name suggests, this is the type of guitar used for classical music, but it is also commonly used for Flamenco, Folk, and World music. Some of the most famous classical guitarists are Andres Segovia, John Williams and Alirio Diaz. American fingerpicker Chet Atkins used an electric classical guitar.

LESSON ELEVEN

Fifth String Notes

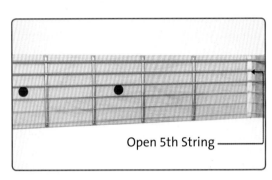

A Note

To play the A note, pick the open **5th** string.

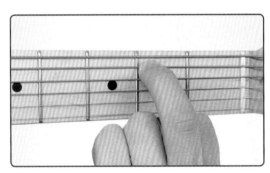

B Note

Play the B note with the **second** finger of your left hand behind the **second** fret of the 5th string.

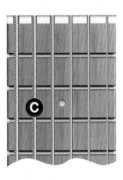
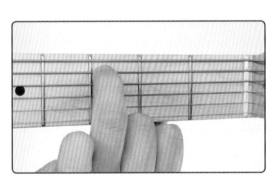

C Note

Play the C note with the **third** finger of your left hand behind the **third** fret of the 5th string.

22.0   Volga Boatman

V V∧V V∧
1   2 + 3   4 +

22.1 Blow the Man Down

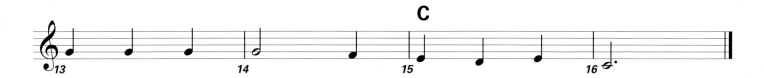

22.2 Harem Dance

Note Summary

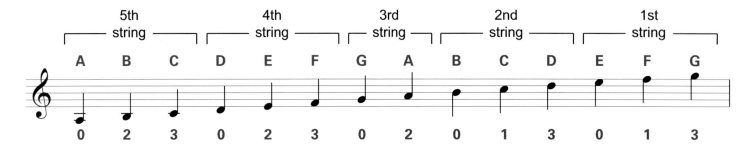

	5th string			4th string			3rd string			2nd string			1st string	
A	B	C	D	E	F	G	A	B	C	D	E	F	G
0	2	3	0	2	3	0	2	0	1	3	0	1	3

Guitar Effects...
The Whammy Bar

The tremolo arm or "Whammy Bar" can be used to produce a variety of sounds on the electric guitar, ranging from subtle vibrato on chords to dramatic bends, harmonics and "dive bombs". There are several different types of whammy bars fitted to all types of electric guitars. These include Fender, Bigsby and Floyd Rose. Use of the whammy bar was first thoroughly explored by Jimi Hendrix who brought many new sounds into music.

Know your Guitars...
National Reso-lectric

This electric resonator guitar is great for playing the Blues. It has the resonator cone which picks up the acoustic sound and gives the guitar it's distinctive tone, as well as an electric pickup so it can be played through an amp. It works equally well for fingerpicking or using a pick. With heavy strings it is extremely suitable for slide playing. By putting lighter strings on this guitar, you can also get great sounds when bending notes.

F Major Chord

F

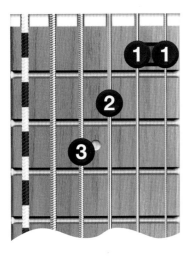

F

To play the **F** chord, use the **first**, **second** and **third** fingers of your left hand as shown in the diagram. Strum only **five** strings. The **first** finger **bars** across the first two strings. This is quite difficult at first. The **F** chord is easier to play if you position your **third** and **second** before positioning the first finger.

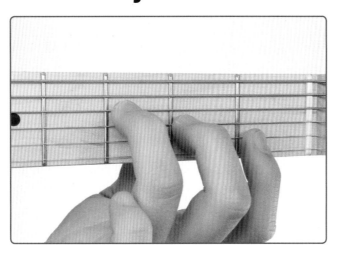

 23.0

$$V_\wedge V_\wedge V_\wedge V$$
$$1 + 2 + 3 + 4$$

Remember that you can use any rhythm pattern you like on any chord progression as long as they have the same time signature e.g. $\frac{4}{4}$ time.

| C | Em | F | G⁷ |

C Seventh Chord

C7

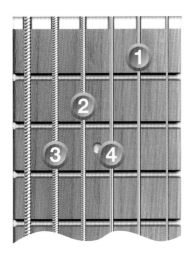

C7

To play the **C7** chord, use the **four** fingers of your left hand as shown in the diagram, and strum all **six** strings. The **C7** chord is a **C** chord with an added **B**♭ note played by the fourth finger.

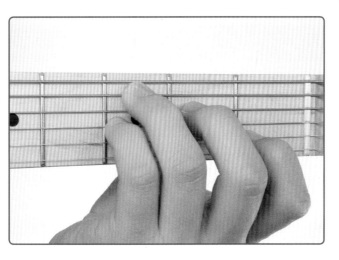

23.1

V∧V∧V V
1 + 2 + 3   4

Use your **second** finger as a **pivot** when changing between the **F** and **Dm chords**. Use your **first** and **second** fingers as **pivots** when changing between **Am** and **C7**.

| F | Dm | Am | C7 |

Turnaround Progressions

In Lesson Four, you were introduced to the 12 bar Blues chord progression. Another important chord progression is the **turnaround**. Like 12 bar Blues, it is the basis of many songs, and it will probably sound familiar to you also. The first chord progression on the previous page is a turnaround in the key of **C major**.

Unlike 12 bar Blues, where the progression occurs over a fixed number of bars, the turnaround progression may vary in length as in the examples below. However, the **chord sequence** remains the same. Some of the biggest hit records of all time are based upon a turnaround progression. Every year since the beginning of Rock there have been hit songs based upon 12 bar Blues or turnarounds.

Some songs that are based upon a turnaround progression are:

Stand by Me - John Lennon
I Will Always Love You - Whitney Housten
Return to Sender - Elvis Presley
All I Have to do is Dream - The Everly Brothers
Crocodile Rock - Elton John
Everlasting Love - U2

Houses of the Holy - Led Zeppelin
Uptown Girl - Billy Joel
Blue Moon - various artists
Tell Me Why - The Beatles
Hungry Heart - Bruce Springsteen

24.0   Turnaround Progression in the Key of G Major

V V V∧V
1   2   3 + 4

| G | Em | C | D7 |

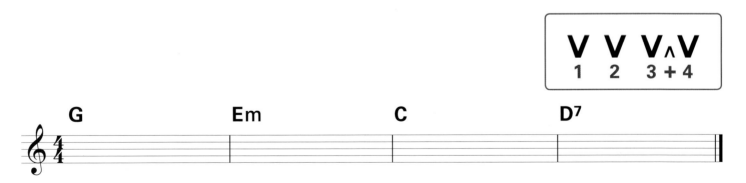

Alternative Chord Fingerings

To make the chord changes in the above progression easier, play the **Em** chord with your **first** and **second** fingers. This will allow the use of **pivot** fingers between **G** to **Em** and **Em** to **C**. A pivot can also be used between **C** and **D7** and a **slide** finger between **G** and **D7**. Alternative fingering for any chord shape can be used to make chord progressions easier to play.

 24.1   Turnaround Progression in the Key of C Major

In this turnaround there are two chords in each bar.
Use your **first** and **second** fingers as **pivots** when changing between **C** and **Am**.

| C | Am | F | G⁷ | C | Am | F | G⁷ |

Notice the similarity in sound between the above two Turnaround progressions.
They are the **same** progression but in two different keys.

Guitar Effects...
Delay Pedal

The delay pedal makes a copy of what a guitarist plays and repeats it at a specific rate depending on how the controls are set. You can control the speed of the delay and the number of repeats. Delays are used to great effect by Edge from U2, David Gilmour of Pink Floyd and Andy Summers of the Police.

LESSON THIRTEEN

Rests

In music, rests are used to indicate periods of silence. For each note value there is a corresponding rest, as outlined in the following table.

	Whole Note	Half Note	Quarter Note
Value	4	2	1
	Whole Rest	Half Rest	Quarter Rest

The Common Time Signature

The $\mathbf{C}$ at the beginning of this exercise stands for **common time**, which is another name for $\frac{4}{4}$ time.

▶ 25.0

V V∧V V∧
1 2 + 3 4 +

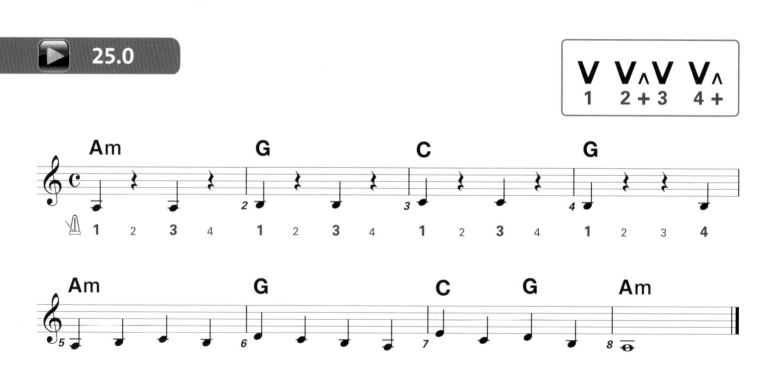

Know your Guitars…
Fender Stratocaster

The Fender Stratocaster is one of the most famous of all electric guitars. Designed by Leo Fender and first released in 1954, the Stratocaster (commonly called a "Strat") has been used by millions of guitarists all over the world. Some of the most famous Strat players include Jimi Hendrix, Mark Knopfler and Eric Clapton.

Sixth String Notes

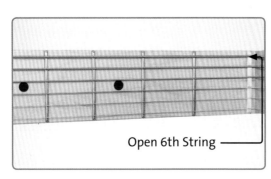

E Note

To play the E note, pick the open **6th** string.

Open 6th String

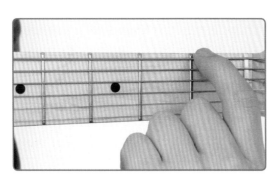

F Note

Play the F note with the **first** finger of your left hand behind the **first** fret of the **6th** string.

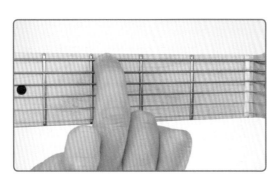

G Note

Play the G note with the **third** finger of your left hand behind the **third** fret of the **6th** string.

 26.0

26.1   I Gave My Love a Cherry

26.2   12 Bar Blues in the Key of C

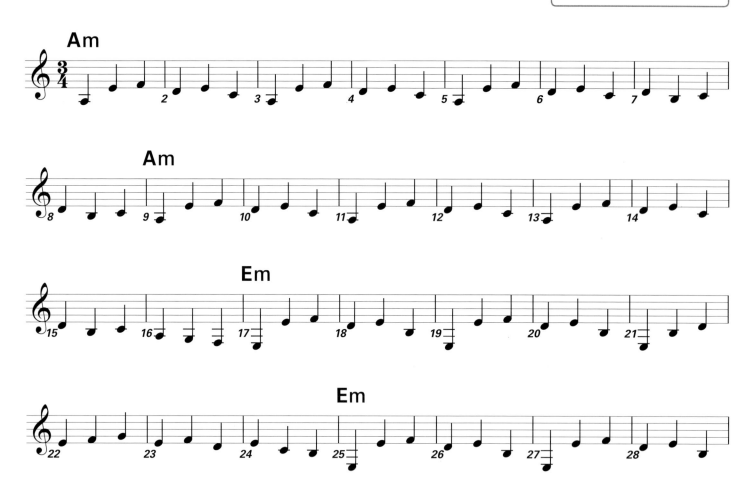

Know your Guitars...
Dobro

The Dobro is a metal bodied "Resonator Guitar". It has a resonator cone which amplifies the sound even though there are no electronics involved. There are also wooden bodied guitars with a metal resonator cone. All these guitars are great for slide and fingerpicking. They are traditionally associated with Blues, Bluegrass, Country and other Roots music.

Open Position Notes

All of the notes you have studied, as summarised below, are in the **open position**.
The open position consists of the open string notes and the notes on the first three frets.

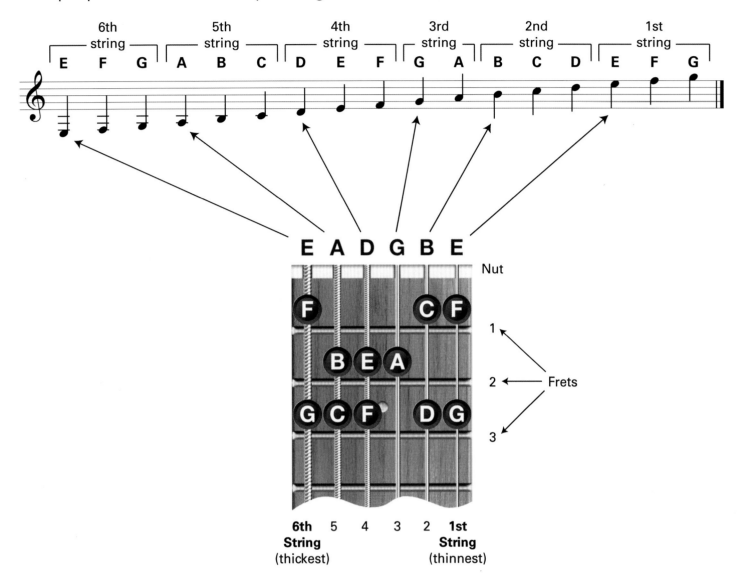

By playing through the notes you will notice **B** to **C** and **E** to **F** are only one fret apart (called a **semitone**), whereas all other notes are two frets apart (called a **tone**). The distance between notes of the musical alphabet can be set out as such:

It is essential for you to remember this pattern of notes.

Troubleshooting
- Revise all songs and exercises so far studied.
- Double-check your timing and smoothness of sound. To do this, try recording yourself.
- Remember to watch the music, **not** the guitar.

LESSON FIFTEEN

Eighth Notes

An **eighth note (or quaver)** ♪ is worth half a count. Two eighth notes, which are usually joined by a line (called a beam) ♫, have the same value as a quarter note.

Eighth notes are counted as such:

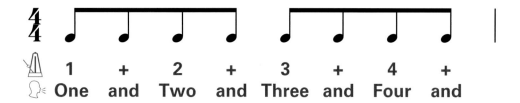

Here is a combination of half notes, quarter notes and eighth notes in ♩ time.

The **eighth note rest** ⅞ , is worth half a count of silence.

Alternate Picking

All of the melodies you have played so far involved a downward pick motion, indicated by V. With the introduction of eighth notes, the technique of down and up (∧) picking is used. This is called **alternate picking**, and it is essential for the development of speed and accuracy.

In alternate picking, use a down pick **on** the beat (the number count) and an up pick **off** the beat (the 'and' count). Try the following exercise:

Amplifiers...
The Fender Twin

The most famous of all combo amps is the Fender Twin Reverb. It produces a crisp clean tone, even at high volumes and is used by players of many different musical styles. Many players use a Fender Twin as their basic sound and combine it with pedals to achieve distortion and other effects.

Duets

It is important for you to be able to play with other musicians and the best practice for this is the study of duets. Duets are written as two independent parts of music, which are indicated by the Roman Numerals at the beginning of each line. In classical music the first guitar is called Primo ($\bar{I}$) and second guitar Secondo ($\bar{II}$).

To get the most benefit from duets practice **both** parts.

Playing duets will present specific problems.

Be careful of the following:

* Make sure to stay on your correct part
  (e.g. either the top or bottom line).
* Pay particular attention to your timing and try not
  to stop if the other guitarist makes a mistake.
* Do not be distracted by the other guitarist's part.

Know your Guitars...
The Fender Telecaster

This classic solid body electric guitar is used extensively in Country music and is also popular with Rock, Pop, Soul, Funk and Blues players. It is capable of producing a variety of sounds from clear bell like tones to stinging attacking sounds. Equally effective for both Rhythm and Lead guitar, the Telecaster has been favored by players like James Burton (who played with Elvis Presley), Muddy Waters, Albert Lee and Roy Buchanan.

LESSON SIXTEEN

Bm

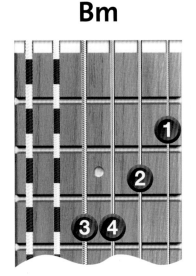

B Minor Chord

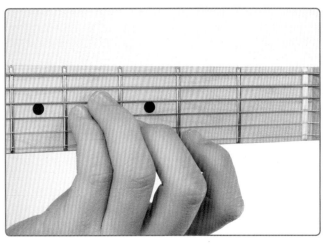

Bm

To play the **Bm** chord, use the **first**, **second**, **third** and **fourth** fingers of your left hand as shown in the diagram. Strum only **four** strings.

The following progression is a turnaround in the key of D major. It contains the **Bm** chord and there are two chords per bar each receiving two counts. Notice that this progression sounds similar to the turnarounds you have already learnt.

▶ 31.0

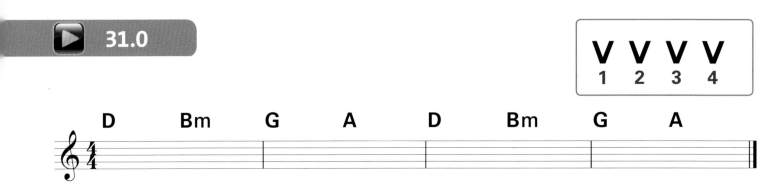

The following turnaround is in the key of **G major**. Each chord is played for two bars.

▶ 31.1

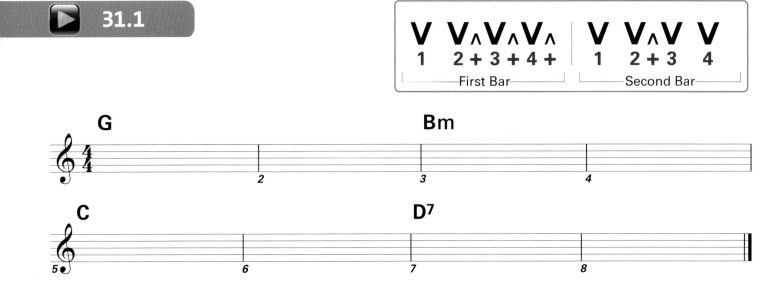

B7

B Seventh Chord

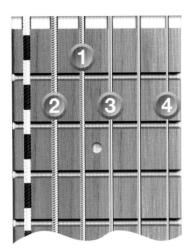

To play the **B7** chord, use all **four** fingers of your left hand as shown in the diagram. Strum only **five** strings.

Some guitarists deaden the 6th string by lightly touching it with the left hand thumb which reaches over the top of the neck. The 6th string can then be strummed but it won't sound as it is deadened. This technique can apply to any chord where the 6th string note is not a part of the chord shape.

 32.0

V∧V∧V∧V
1 + 2 + 3 + 4

| A | B⁷ | D | E⁷ |

 32.1

V V V∧V
1 2 3 + 4

| Em | D⁷ | C⁷ | B⁷ |

 32.2

V V V∧V
1 2 3 + 4

This progression contains both **B7** and **Bm**.

| G | B⁷ | Em | G⁷ |
| 1 | 2 | 3 | 4 |

| C | Bm | Am | D⁷ | G |
| 5 | 6 | 7 | | 8 |

LESSON SEVENTEEN

Sharps

A sharp (♯) is a sign, placed immediately **before** a note, which raises the pitch of that note by **one semitone (one fret)**. When you see a note with a sharp sign in front of it, you should first think of where the normal note is located (in music this is called the **natural** note), and then sharpen it by placing your **next finger** on the **next fret** along. Here are some examples:

C♯	F♯	G♯	C♯
2nd String	1st String	3rd String	5th String
2nd Fret	2nd Fret	1st Fret	4th Fret
2nd Finger	2nd Finger	1st Finger	4th Finger

The use of the sharp sign introduces five new notes, occurring in between the seven natural notes which you already know. The following exercise outlines all twelve notes which occur within one octave of music. Play through it **very slowly**, and be sure to use correct fingering for the sharpened notes.

▶ 33.0

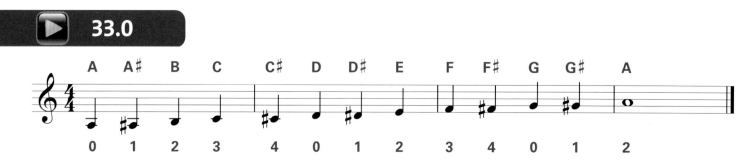

You will notice that there is no sharp between **B** and **C**, or between **E** and **F**.
The exercise you have just played is called a **chromatic scale**. It is referred to as the **A chromatic scale** because the starting and finishing notes are **A** (this is called the **Key note** or **tonic**).
The chromatic scale consists entirely of **semitones** i.e. it moves up (or down) one fret at a time.

▶ 33.1

Here is the **G** chromatic scale:

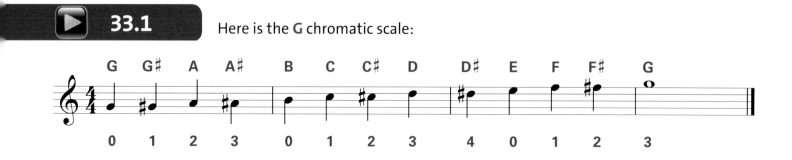

When a note is sharpened it **remains** sharp until either a **bar line** or a **natural sign** (♮) cancels it. Check the following notes:

34   House of the Rising Sun

35   Dark Eyes

Watch your timing with the ties in this song.

Troubleshooting

- Be sure to use the correct fingering for all notes:
  - 1st fret .... 1st finger
  - 2nd fret .... 2nd finger
  - 3rd fret .... 3rd finger
  - 4th fret .... 4th finger

- Keep your left hand fingers as close to the strings as possible.
  This will greatly improve your accuracy and speed.

- **Watch** the music and **read** the notes.
  Occasionally you should just name the notes in a song, without actually playing through it.

LESSON EIGHTEEN

Flats

A **flat** (♭) is a sign, placed immediately **before** a note, which **lowers** the pitch of that note by one semitone. Locate the following flats:

When an open string note is flattened, the new note must be located on the **next lower string** e.g.:

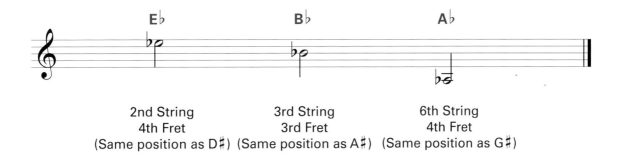

2nd String	3rd String	6th String
4th Fret	3rd Fret	4th Fret
(Same position as D♯)	(Same position as A♯)	(Same position as G♯)

You will notice that it is possible for the same note (in pitch) to have two different names. For example, F♯ = G♭ and G♯ = A♭. These are referred to as **enharmonic** notes. The following fretboard diagram outlines all of the notes in the **first position** on the guitar (including both names for the enharmonic notes). The first position consists of the open string notes and the notes on the first four frets.

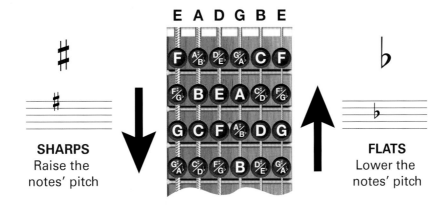

Here are two octaves of the **E chromatic scale**, ascending using sharps and descending using flats.

As with sharps, flats are cancelled by a bar line or by a natural sign.

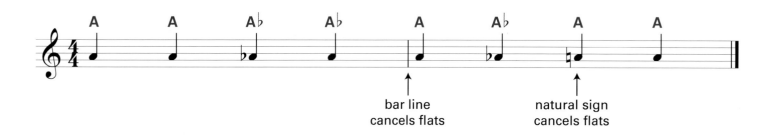

bar line
cancels flats

natural sign
cancels flats

Electric Guitar Pickups…
Single Coil Pickups

Electric guitars contain pickups which capture the sound coming from the strings and send the signal to the amplifier. The original pickups were single coil pickups similar to the one shown here. These pickups are commonly found in Fender guitars like the Stratocaster which contains three single coil pickups, and the Telecaster which contains two different single coil pickups.

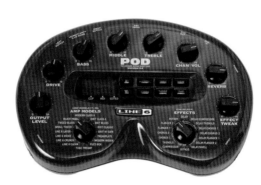

Guitar Effects…
The Pod

The Line 6 Pod is a portable amp simulator for guitar. You can plug any electric guitar into it and by changing the settings, you can emulate the sound of the guitar being played through many different amps. The sounds range from Traditional Fender and Vox amps to Marshall stacks, through to high gain modern Mesa Boogie amps.

Know your Guitars…
The Flying V

This dramatic looking guitar was first released by Gibson in 1958. Like the Les Paul, it contains two humbucking pickups and is great for playing Rock, Blues and Metal. It was used extensively by Bluesmen Albert King and Lonnie Mack, as well as Jimi Hendrix. A later version released by Jackson was used by Randy Rhoads when he was Ozzy Ozborne's lead guitarist. Today there are many different Flying V style guitars available.

First and Second Endings

This song introduces **first** and **second endings (see Line 6)**. On the first time through, ending **one** is played, as indicated by the bracket: ⌐1. ⌐

The section of music is then repeated (go back to the beginning of line 5) and on the second time ending **two** is played. Be careful **not** to play both endings together.

39   Hall of the Mountain King

If you are playing the chords to this song it is easier to play the **G♭7**, **F7** and **B** chords as **bar chords.**
To learn how to play bar chords see Progressive Guitar Method: Bar Chords.

LESSON NINETEEN

Silent Strums and Continuous Rhythm

The basic $\frac{4}{4}$ rhythm pattern learnt in Lesson Three consisted of four down strums, i.e.

$$\begin{array}{cccc} \mathbf{V} & \mathbf{V} & \mathbf{V} & \mathbf{V} \\ 1 & 2 & 3 & 4 \end{array}$$

After playing the first strum, your right hand moves upwards in preparation for the second strum. The strings are not played on this upward movement. This upward motion can be represented by a broken upward strum symbol (Λ·) which indicates that the strings are not strummed (a silent strum).

So the basic rhythm above could be written as:

$$\begin{array}{cccccccc} \mathbf{V} & \mathbf{\Lambda} & \mathbf{V} & \mathbf{\Lambda} & \mathbf{V} & \mathbf{\Lambda} & \mathbf{V} & \mathbf{\Lambda} \\ 1 & + & 2 & + & 3 & + & 4 & + \end{array}$$

The above two rhythm patterns sound exactly the same.

If you watch your **right** hand you will notice that it actually moves **up and down** in a **continuous motion** but it only makes contact with the strings on the **down** strum.

Also when you play eighth note rhythms you will see that your right hand also moves up and down in a continuous motion sometimes making contact with the string and sometimes not.

Silent Strum Symbols

When an **upward** strum is made without contacting the strings it can be represented by Λ·.

When a **downward** strum is made without contacting the strings it can be represented by V̇.

Some very useful and interesting rhythm patterns can result by incorporating eighth note rhythms with silent down strums. V̇

 40.0

Try the following rhythm holding a **C** chord.

This rhythm is the same as eighth note rhythm pattern 2 in Lesson Six, except the down strum on the third beat does not make contact with the strings. Practice this rhythm until you perfect it.
You can apply it to any chord progression you like. This is a very important rhythm and will be the basis of many other rhythms.
Apply this rhythm pattern to the following chord progression. Use pivot and slide fingers where possible to make the chord changes easier.

40.1

C   Am   Dm   G⁷

Try a variation of this rhythm pattern on the following turnaround progression in the key of G.
To make the chord changes easier use the alternative fingerings on page 53.

 40.2

G   Em   C   D

The following variation has a silent **down** strum on the 2nd and 3rd beat.
Apply it to the progression below.

 40.3

When changing between **C** and **A7** use your **second** finger as a pivot.

C   A⁷   D⁷   G⁷

Rhythm Variations

Try the following rhythm variations and make up your own. Apply these rhythms to any chord progression you like. A **G** chord is used on the recording. All these suggested variations are in $\frac{4}{4}$ time but the same principle can be applied to $\frac{3}{4}$ time. Also note that in all these rhythms your **right** hand moves up and down in a **continuous motion**. These rhythm patterns can sound "off the beat". This is called **syncopation**.

 41.0-41.5

41.0

41.1

41.2

41.3

41.4

41.5

42   Blues Traveller

43   Blue Seas

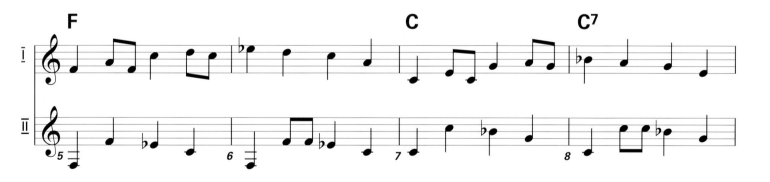

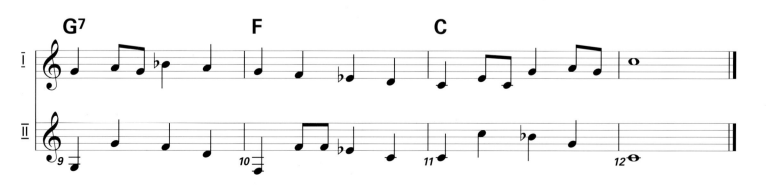

LESSON TWENTY

Dotted Quarter Notes

A **dotted quarter note** is worth 1½ counts. It has the same time value as a quarter note tied to an eighth note, i.e.

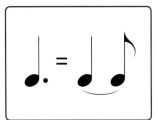

When a dotted quarter note is followed by an eighth note, as in Greensleeves, the count is as follows:

▶ 44   Greensleeves

This song features some difficult left hand fingering passages which will require special attention. In any music you play, be sure to **isolate** difficult sections and practice them thoroughly.

The eighth notes in Greensleeves are played with an up pick, as indicated.

The 'High' A Note

The **'high' A note** is located on the 5th fret of the first string, and is played using the **fourth** finger.

45.0 Practice the following exercise slowly and carefully. Watch the music!

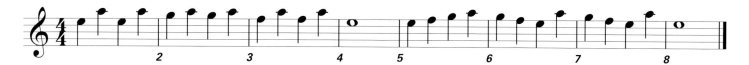

45.1 Scarborough Fair

Scarborough Fair uses the high **A** note in bars 6, 8 and 9. The abbreviation **rit**, in bar 15, stands for **ritardando**, which means to **gradually slow down**.

Accessories...
The Capo

The capo is a device which is placed across the neck of the guitar (acting as a moveable nut). This enables you to change the key of a song without changing the chord shapes. It also allows you to play easier chord shapes for songs in difficult keys. To learn how to use a capo, see Complete Learn to Play Rhythm Guitar or Complete Learn to Play Fingerpicking Guitar.

LESSON TWENTY-ONE

Suspended Chords

The chord symbol for a suspended chord is the major chord symbol plus the word **sus** (or sometimes **sus4**). The suspended chord is quite often used to add interest to a progression if there is a long section of music containing only one chord.

Dsus

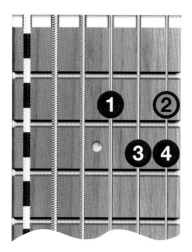

D Suspended

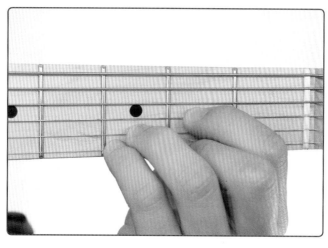

Dsus

Hold a **D major** chord shape then place your **fourth** finger on the **third** fret of the **1st** string.

The **open circle** on the chord diagram indicates that you hold the major chord shape and add the suspended note with your **fourth** finger. Suspended chords are nearly always played just before or just after the major chord, so it is easier to change between them if the major chord shape is held in position.

47.0

$$V_\wedge V_\wedge \bar{V}_\wedge V_\wedge$$
1 + 2 + 3 + 4 +

| D | Dsus | D | Dsus |

Asus

A Suspended

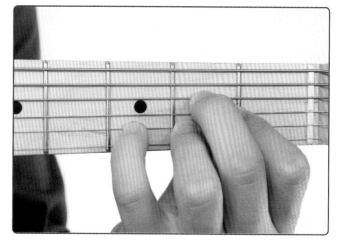

Asus

Hold an **A major** chord shape then place your **fourth** finger on the **third** fret of the **2nd** string.

47.1

| A | Asus | A | Asus |

Esus

E Suspended

Esus

Hold an **E major** chord shape then place your **fourth** finger on the **second** fret of the **3rd** string.

47.2

This progression is two bars long. Change to the **E sus** chord (i.e. add your fourth finger) on the '**+**' after the 3 count.

Change here

| E | Esus | E | Esus |

The next progression contains all three of the above **sus** chords. Change to the **sus** chord on the '**+**' after the 2 count. Use **pivot** and **slide** fingers wherever possible between chord changes.

47.3

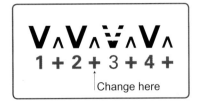

Change here

| A | Asus | A | Asus | D | Dsus | D | Dsus |
| E | Esus | E | Esus | A | Asus | A | Asus |

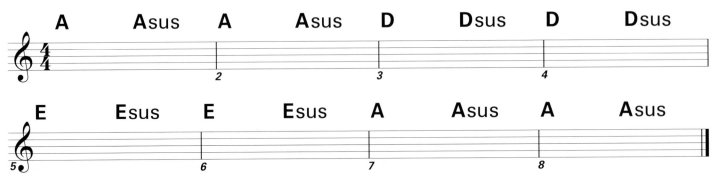

Here is a melody accompanied by the **sus** chords you have just learnt.

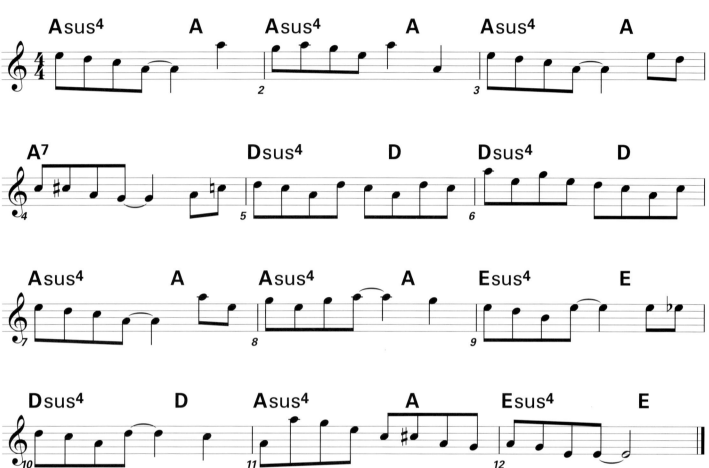

Guitar Effects...
Overdrive and Distortion

One of the great sounds you can make with an electric guitar and an amp is Overdrive or Distortion. This is usually achieved with the help of a pedal which you plug into on the way to the amp. The one shown here is an Ibanez Tube Screamer. There are many distortion pedals available with names like Metal Zone, Super Distortion and Fuzz Box. Try some out at a music store.

LESSON TWENTY-TWO

More on Bass Note Rhythm Patterns

In lesson 9 you were introduced to bass note rhythm patterns in $\frac{3}{4}$ time. When playing a progression in $\frac{4}{4}$ time the following bass note rhythm patterns are commonly used.

Pick the bass note of the chord on the first beat and strum the first three or four strings of the chord on the 2nd, 3rd and 4th beats. Play the following bass note rhythm pattern holding a **G** chord shape.

 49.0

The best bass note to pick is the lowest note of the chord that has the same letter name of the chord. This is called the root note.

When playing a **G** type, pick the **6th** string note (**G note**), eg. G and G7 chords
When playing a **D** type, pick the **4th** string note (**D note**), eg. D, D7 and Dm chords
When playing a **C** type, pick the **5th** string note (**C note**), eg. C and C7 chords
When playing an **A** type, pick the **5th** string note (**A note**), eg. A, A7 and Am
When playing an **E** type, pick the **6th** string note (**E note**), eg. E, E7 and Em chords
When playing a **F** type, pick the **4th** string note (**F note**), eg. F chord

Practice this rhythm technique on each chord separately at first.
Remember to hold the full chord shape even though you are not playing all the strings.

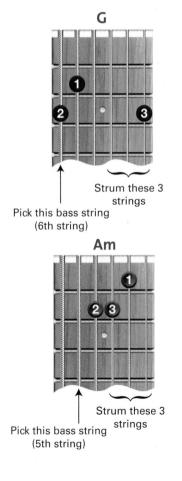

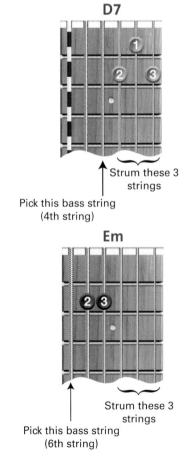

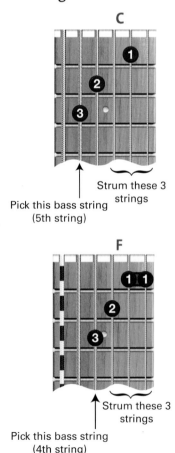

Play the following turnaround progression using bass note rhythm pattern 1.
Play the root note of the first beat of each bar.

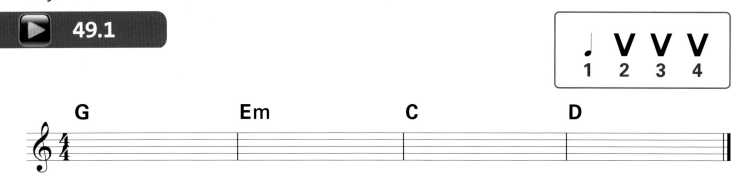

Now try a chord progression using a variation of bass note rhythm pattern 1 which contains **eighth** note strums on the second beat.

Bass Note Rhythm Pattern
Variation 1

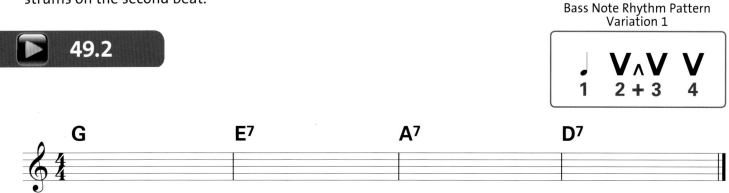

Bass Note Rhythm Pattern
Variation 2

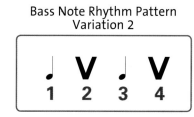

Another variation is to play the bass note on the first and third beats and strum on the second and fourth beats. Play the following bass note strum rhythm pattern, also holding a **G** chord shape. Play the root note of the chord on the first and third beats of the bar.

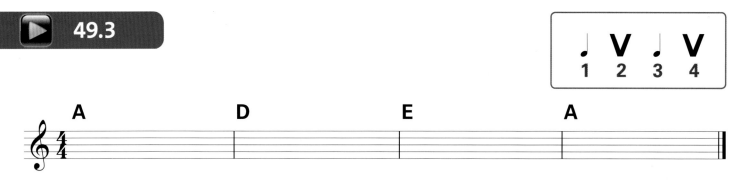

Apply the above variation to the following chord progression which contains two chords in each bar.

PROGRESSIVE GUITAR METHOD BOOK 1: Notes, Chords and Rhythms

Once you are comfortable playing bass note rhythm patterns, try using this technique to accompany the following melody.

 50　　**Arkansas Traveller**

Guitar Setups...
Pickup Combinations

The electric guitars of the 1950's and 60's traditionally had either single coil pickups or humbuckers. Although both companies had exceptions, Fender guitars like the Stratocaster and Telecaster usually had single coil pickups, while Gibson guitars like the Les Paul and the 335 had humbuckers. In the 1970's people began to experiment with both types of pickups on the same guitar. Today there are many guitar manufacturers using the single, single, humbucker combination shown here, making the guitar far more versatile.

Alternate Bass Note Picking

In the previous examples the same bass note (the root note) is picked on the first and third beats. Another way of playing bass note picking is to alternate the bass notes. This rhythm is commonly used in Country music. You can alternate between any bass notes that are in the chord shapes. As long as you hold the chord shape while picking the bass notes it will sound correct. Certain bass notes will sound better with certain chords. The best notes to use are the ones that sound good to your ear. It is usual to pick the root note on the first beat followed by a different bass note on the third beat. Use alternate bass note picking in the following chord progression. You can also experiment playing different bass notes than the ones suggested.

51.0

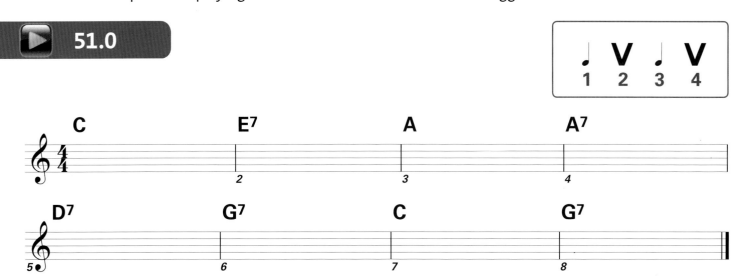

For the **C**, **A7** and **A** chords alternate the bass from the 5th string to the 4th string.

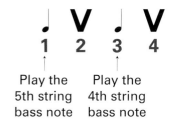

For the **D7** chord alternate between the 4th string bass note and the 5th string bass note.

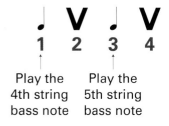

For the **G7** and **E7** chords alternate between the 6th string bass note and the 4th string bass note.

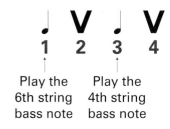

Practice each chord shape separately at first and experiment using alternate bass note picking on other progressions.

51.1 **God Rest Ye Merry Gentlemen**

When playing the accompaniment to this song, you could use an alternate bass note on the third beat of each bar.

Know your Guitars…
Gibson 335

Many Blues and Jazz players favor hollow body electric guitars for their full, rich tone. One of the most famous hollow body electrics is the Gibson 335. It has been used by players like Freddy King, Magic Sam and Larry Carlton. BB King had a model called the 345 specially designed for him. His guitar is named Lucille.

The Major Scale

The **major scale** is a series of **8** notes in alphabetical order that has the familiar sound:

| Do | Re | Mi | Fa | So | La | Ti | Do |

The **C major scale** contains the following notes.

Note Name	C		D		E	F		G		A		B	C
Interval		tone		tone	semitone		tone		tone		tone	semitone	
		T		T	ST		T		T		T	ST	

The distance between each note is two frets except for **EF** and **BC** where the distance is only one fret.

The distance of two frets is called a **tone** (sometimes called a **step**), indicated by **T**.

The distance of one fret is called a **semitone** (sometimes called a **half step**), indicated by **S**.

The first note and last note of a major scale always have the same name.
In the **C major** scale the distance from the lowest C to the C note above it is **one octave** (8 notes).
The following example is one octave of the C major scale.

 52.0   **The C Major Scale**

| C | D | E | F | G | A | B | C |

Each of the 8 notes in the major scale is given a **scale number** (or **degree**)

Note Name	C		D		E	F		G		A		B	C
Interval		tone		tone	semitone		tone		tone		tone	semitone	
		T		T	ST		T		T		T	ST	

The distance between two notes is called an **interval**.

In any major scale the interval between the 3rd to 4th note and the 7th to 8th note in the scale is one semitone (1 fret) apart. All other notes are one tone (2 frets) apart.

The Key Of C Major

When a song consists of notes from a particular scale, it is said to be written in the **key** which has the same notes as that scale. For example, if a song contains mostly notes from the **C major scale**, it is said to be in the **key of C major**. The songs you have played in this book that commence with a **C** chord written above the first bar of music are in the **key of C major**.

V V ∧ V
1 2 + 3

Morning Has Broken is a well known folk song. It is written here in the key of **C major**.

In any particular key, certain chords are more common than others, and after a while you will become familiar with the chords that belong to each key. Certain keys are easier for guitarists to play in and you should learn how to transpose (change the key of a song) so you can change a song that is in a difficult key (contains lots of sharps and flats or difficult chord shapes for a beginner to play) into an easier key. The most common chords in the key of C major are;

C   Dm   Em   F   G7   Am

For more information on transposing and chords, see Progressive Guitar Method: Rhythm.

Know your Guitars...
Acoustic Cutaway

As well as the standard acoustic guitar, there is another version called a Cutaway where part of the body of the guitar is cut back and reshaped along the side of the fretboard. This makes it easier to play notes high up on the fretboard, which is great for playing Lead solos on an acoustic guitar. Many players who switch frequently between acoustic and electric prefer to use an acoustic cutaway.

LESSON TWENTY-FOUR

The G Major Scale

The **G major** scale starts and ends on the note **G** and contains an **F sharp** (**F♯**) note. Written below are two octaves of the **G major** scale. Notice that the **G major** scale has the same patterns of tones and semitones as the **C major** scale. In a major scale the interval between the 3rd to 4th note and the 7th to 8th notes is a semitone (1 fret). In the **G major** scale, to keep this pattern of tones and semitones correct, an F♯ note must be used instead of an F note.

 53.0   The G Major Scale over Two Octaves

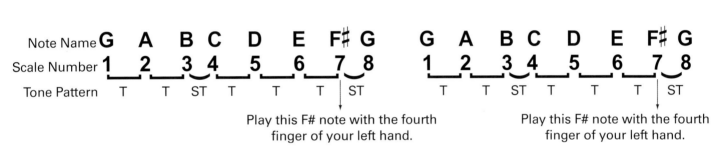

Note Name	G	A	B	C	D	E	F♯	G		G	A	B	C	D	E	F♯	G
Scale Number	1	2	3	4	5	6	7	8		1	2	3	4	5	6	7	8
Tone Pattern	T		T	ST	T	T	T	ST		T		T	ST	T	T	T	ST

Play this F# note with the fourth finger of your left hand.   Play this F# note with the fourth finger of your left hand.

Songs in the key of C major use notes from the C major scale, songs in the key of G major use notes from the G major scale, so songs in the key of G major will contain F sharp (F♯) notes rather than F.

Key Signatures

Instead of writing a sharp sign before every F note on the staff, it is easier to write just one sharp sign after each clef. This means that all the F notes on the staff are played as F♯, even though there is no sharp sign written before them.
This is called a **key signature**.

C Major Key signature

The **C major** scale contains no sharps or flats, therefore the key signature for the key of **C major** contains no sharps or flats.

G Major Key signature

The **G major** scale contains one sharp, F♯, therefore the key signature for the key of **G major** contains one sharp, F♯.

The most common chords in the key of G major are;

G   Am   Bm   C   D7   Em

The following songs 'All Through the Night' and 'Lavender's Blue' are in the key of G major.
The key signature tells you that all F notes on the music are played as F sharp (F♯).

These songs contain all the common chords in the key of G major.

The F Major Scale

All major scales have the same pattern of tones and semitones, i.e. the interval between the 3rd and 4th note and the 7th to 8th note in the scale is a semitone (1 fret). For the **F major** scale to keep this pattern of tones and semitones a **B flat** (B♭)note must be used instead of a **B** note.

54.0   The F Major Scale over Two Octaves

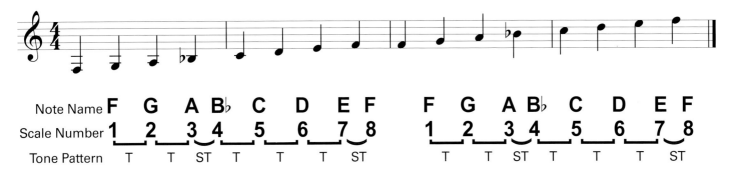

Note Name	F	G	A	B♭	C	D	E	F		F	G	A	B♭	C	D	E	F
Scale Number	1	2	3	4	5	6	7	8		1	2	3	4	5	6	7	8
Tone Pattern	T		T	ST	T		T		T	ST	T		T	ST	T		T		T		T	ST

Songs in the key of F major use notes from the F major scale, so songs in the key of F major will contain B flat (B♭) notes rather than B.

F Major Key signature

The **F major** scale contains one flat B♭, therefore the key signature for the key of **F major** contains one flat, B♭.

The most common chords in the key of F major are;

F   Gm   Am   B♭   C7   Dm

54.1   The Galway Piper

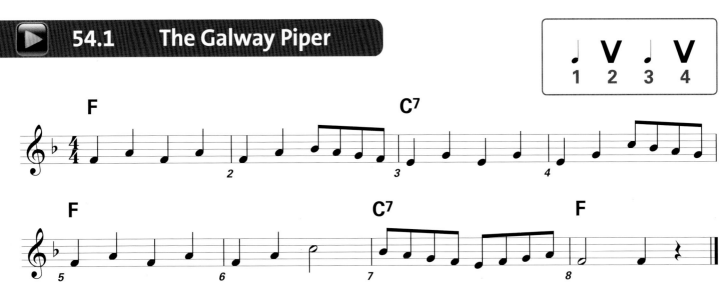

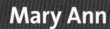

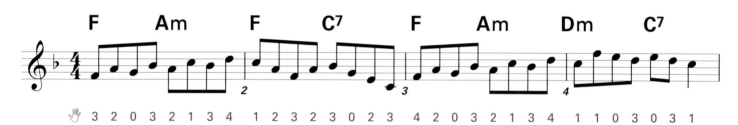

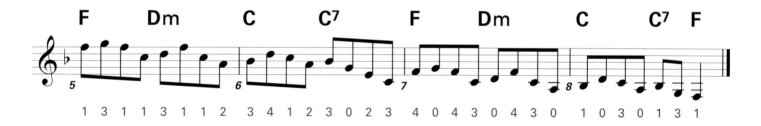

Know your Guitars…

Gibson Les Paul

Along with the Fender Stratocaster, the Gibson Les Paul is one of the most famous of all electric guitars. It is great for heavy Rock sounds as well as as being versatile enough for Blues and Jazz. This guitar was made specially for Les Paul - a great Jazz player who also invented multitrack recording. This technique is essential for recording and is now used by everyone from top recording studios to musicians using computers at home.

LESSON TWENTY-SIX

The Eighth Rest

This symbol is an **eighth rest.** It indicates **half a beat** of silence.

▶ 55.0

There are two common positions for eighth note rests: off the beat and on the beat. These are demonstrated in the following example.

Syncopation

Syncopation occurs when notes are played "off" the beat, i.e. when notes are not played on the number part of the count but on the '+' part of the count.

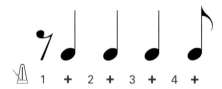

A tie can also be used to create a syncopated feel, by moving the accent (emphasis) off the beat.

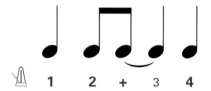

The syncopation in the following songs is created by using both of the above methods.

► 55.1   Elemental Syncopation Blues

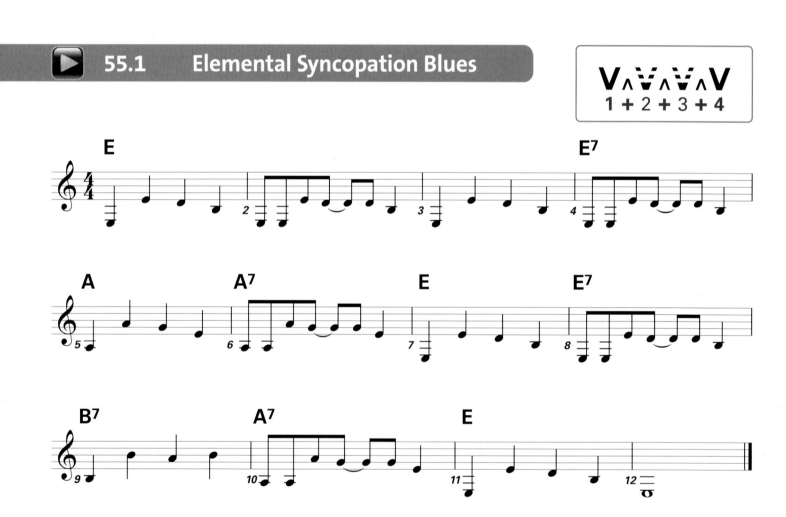

Electric Guitar Pickups…
Humbuckers

Although single coil pickups make a great sound, they can also produce unwanted noise known as hum. In the 1950's, guitar makers discovered that if you put two single coil pickups together, the second one cancels the hum, as well as producing a fatter, warmer sound. Thus the humbucking pickup (Humbucker) was born. These pickups are traditionally associated with Gibson guitars such as the Les Paul and the 335.

APPENDICES

APPENDIX ONE	Tuning
APPENDIX TWO	Notes on the Guitar Fretboard
APPENDIX THREE	Glossary of Musical Terms

Appendix One - Tuning

It is essential for your guitar to be in tune, so that the chords and notes you play will sound correct. The main problem with tuning for most beginning students is that the ear is not able to determine slight differences in pitch. For this reason you should seek the aid of a teacher or an experienced guitarist. Several methods can be used to tune the guitar. These include:

1. Tuning to another musical instrument such as a piano or another guitar.
2. Tuning to pitch pipes or a tuning fork.
3. Tuning the guitar to itself.
4. Using an electronic tuner.

The most common and useful of these is tuning the guitar to itself. This method involves finding notes of the same pitch on different strings. The adjacent diagram outlines the notes used:

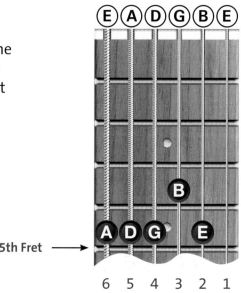

The method of tuning is as follows:

1. Tune the open sixth string to either:
   (a) The open sixth string of another guitar.
   (b) A piano.

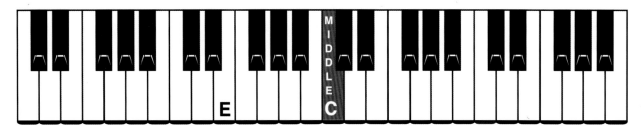

The piano key equivalent to the open 6th string is indicated on the diagram above.

(c) Pitch pipes, which produce notes that correspond with each of the 6 open strings.

(d) A tuning fork. Most tuning forks give the note A.

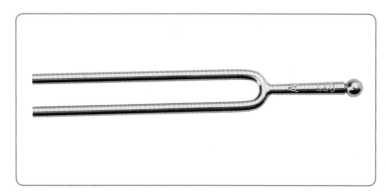

To produce sound from the tuning fork, hold it by the stem and tap one of the prongs against something hard. This will set up a vibration, which can be heard clearly when the bass of the stem is then placed on a solid surface, e.g. a guitar body.

2. Place a finger on the 6th string at the fifth fret. Now play the open A (5th string). If the guitar is to be in tune, then these two notes must have the same pitch (i.e. sound the same). If they do not sound the same, the 5th string must be adjusted to match the note produced on the 6th string, i.e. it is tuned in relation to the 6th string.

3. Tune the open 4th string to the note on the fifth fret of the 5th string, using the method outlined above.

4. Tune all other strings using the same procedure, remembering that the open B string (2nd) is tuned to the 4th fret (check diagram) while all other strings are tuned to the 5th fret.

5. Strum an open E major chord, to check if your guitar is tuned correctly. At first may have some difficulty deciding whether or not the chord sound is correct, but as your ear improves you will become more familiar with the correct sound of the chord.

Tuning may take you many months to master, and you should practice it constantly. The guidance of a teacher will be an invaluable aid in the early stages of guitar tuning.

Tuning Hints

One of the easiest ways to practice tuning is to actually start with the guitar in tune and then de-tune one string. When you do this, always take the string **down** in pitch (i.e. loosen it) as it is easier to tune "up" to a given note rather than "down" to it. As an example, de-tune the 4th string (D). If you strum a chord now, the guitar will sound out of tune, even though only one string has been altered (so remember that if your guitar is out of tune it may only be one string at fault).

Following the correct method, you must tune the 4th string against the D note at the fifth fret of the 5th string. Play the note loudly, and listen carefully to the sound produced. This will help you retain the correct pitch in your mind when tuning the next string.

Now that you have listened carefully to the note that you want, the D string must be tuned to it. Play the D string, and turn its tuning key at the same time, and you will hear the pitch of the string change (it will become higher as the tuning key tightens the string). It is important to follow this procedure, so that you hear the sound of the string at all times, as it tightens. You should also constantly refer back to the correct sound that is required (i.e. the D note on the fifth fret of the 5th string).

Electronic Tuners

Electronic tuners make tuning your guitar very easy. They allow you to tune each string individually to the tuner, by indicating whether the notes are sharp (too high) or flat (too low). It is still recommended however, that you practice tuning your guitar by the above method to help improve your musicianship.

Electronic Tuner

Tuning Your Guitar to the CD or DVD

The DVDs, DVD-ROM and CD contain recordings of the open strings of a guitar. Each string is played several times, giving you sufficient time to tune the corresponding string on your guitar to the sound of the note on the recording. You may also be able to program your player to repeat a specific track several times, increasing the amount of times the note can be heard. The recording contains open string tuning notes for steel string acoustic and electric guitars. Beginners may find it easier to tune the strings of their guitar to the corresponding type of guitar on the recording. Each type of guitar has its own particular tonal characteristics and first time tuners will be able to hear the sound of a string that best matches the sound of their instrument. As with all tuning methods, make sure you practice tuning to the recording in a quiet environment and double check that you are adjusting the correct tuning key before turning.

Appendix Two – Chord Chart

All the chords used throughout this book can be found in the chord chart below. For a complete knowledge of chords and rhythm techniques see Progressive Guitar Method: Rhythm and Progressive Guitar Method: Chords by Gary Turner.

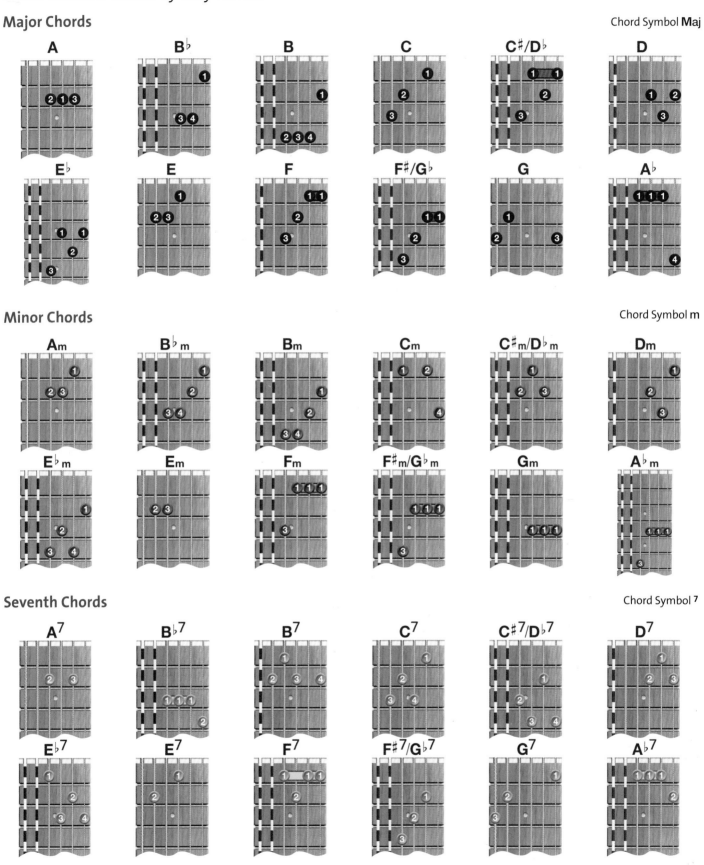

Major Chords

Chord Symbol **Maj**

A   B♭   B   C   C♯/D♭   D

E♭   E   F   F♯/G♭   G   A♭

Minor Chords

Chord Symbol **m**

Am   B♭m   Bm   Cm   C♯m/D♭m   Dm

E♭m   Em   Fm   F♯m/G♭m   Gm   A♭m

Seventh Chords

Chord Symbol **7**

A⁷   B♭⁷   B⁷   C⁷   C♯⁷/D♭⁷   D⁷

E♭⁷   E⁷   F⁷   F♯⁷/G♭⁷   G⁷   A♭⁷

1 indicates 1st finger   **3** indicates 3rd finger   A broken line indicates that a string is not to be played.

2 indicates 2nd finger   **4** indicates 4th finger

Glossary of Musical Terms

Accidental — a sign used to show a temporary change in pitch of a note (i.e. sharp♯, flat♭, double sharp 𝄪, double flat ♭♭, or natural ♮). The sharps or flats in a key signature are not regarded as accidentals.

Ad lib — to be played at the performer's own discretion.

Allegretto — moderately fast.

Allegro — fast and lively.

Anacrusis — a note or notes occurring before the first bar of music (also called 'lead-in' notes).

Andante — an easy walking pace.

Arpeggio — the playing of a chord in single note fashion.

Bar — a division of music occurring between two bar lines (also called a 'measure').

Bar chord — a chord played with one finger lying across all six strings.

Bar line — a vertical line drawn across the staff which divides the music into equal sections called bars.

Bass — the lower regions of pitch in general. On keyboard, the notes to the left of the keyboard.

Capo — a device placed across the neck of a guitar to allow a key change without alteration of the chord shapes.

Chord — a combination of three or more different notes played together.

Chord progression — a series of chords played as a musical unit (e.g. as in a song).

Chromatic scale — a scale ascending and descending in semitones.

e.g. **C** chromatic scale:

ascending: C   C♯   D   D♯   E   F   F♯   G   G♯   A   A♯   B   C

descending: C   B   B♭   A   A♭   G   G♭   F   E   E♭   D   D♭   C

Clef — a sign placed at the beginning of each staff of music which fixes the location of a particular note on the staff, and hence the location of all other notes, e.g.

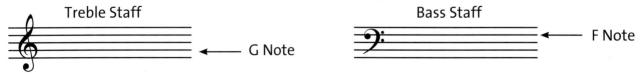

Coda — an ending section of music, signified by the sign ⊕ .

Common time — and indication of ⁴⁄₄ time — four quarter note beats per bar (also indicated by 𝄴)

D.C. al fine — a repeat from the sign (indicated thus 𝄋) to the word 'fine'.

Duration — the time value of each note.

Dynamics — the varying degrees of softness (indicated by the term 'piano') and loudness (indicated by the term 'forte') in music.

Eighth note — a note with the value of half a beat in $\frac{4}{4}$ time, indicated thus ♪ (also called a quaver).

The eighth note rest — indicating half a beat of silence is written: ⅞

Enharmonic — describes the difference in notation, but not in pitch, of two notes: e.g.

F♯ or G♭

Fermata — a sign, ⌢ , used to indicate that a note or chord is held to the player's own discretion (also called a 'pause sign').

First and second endings — signs used where two different endings occur. On the first time through ending one is played (indicated by the bracket ⌐1. ⌐); then the progression is repeated and ending two is played (indicated ⌐2. ⌐).

Flat — a sign, (♭)used to lower the pitch of a note by one semitone.

Forte — loud. Indicated by the sign $\boldsymbol{f}$.

Half note — a note with the value of two beats in $\frac{4}{4}$ time, indicated thus: ♩ (also called a minim). The half note rest, indicating two beats of silence, is written: ▬ on the third staff line.

Harmonics — a chime like sound created by lightly touching a vibrating string at certain points along the fret board.

Harmony — the simultaneous sounding of two or more different notes.

Improvise — to perform spontaneously; i.e. not from memory or from a written copy.

Interval — the distance between any two notes of different pitches.

Key — describes the notes used in a composition in regards to the major or minor scale from which they are taken; e.g. a piece 'in the key of C major' describes the melody, chords, etc., as predominantly consisting of the notes, **C, D, E, F, G, A,** and **B** — i.e. from the **C** scale.

Key signature — a sign, placed at the beginning of each stave of music, directly after the clef, to indicate the key of a piece. The sign consists of a certain number of sharps or flats, which represent the sharps or flats found in the scale of the piece's key. e.g.

indicates a scale with **F♯** and **C♯**, which is **D** major; **D E F♯ G A B C♯ D.**
Therefore the key is **D** major (or its relative minor, Bm).

Lead-In — same as anacrusis (also called a pick-up).

Leger lines — small horizontal lines upon which notes are written when their pitch is either above or below the range of the staff, e.g.

Legato — smoothly, well connected.

Lyric — words that accompany a melody.

Major scale — a series of eight notes in alphabetical order based on the interval sequence tone - tone - semitone - tone - tone - tone - semitone, giving the familiar sound **do re mi fa so la ti do**.

Melody — a succession of notes of varying pitch and duration, and having a recognizable musical shape.

Metronome — a device which indicates the number of beats per minute, and which can be adjusted in accordance to the desired tempo.

e.g. **MM** (Maelzel Metronome) ♩ = 60 — indicates 60 quarter note beats per minute.

Moderato — at a moderate pace.

Natural — a sign (♮)used to cancel out the effect of a sharp or flat. The word is also used to describe the notes **A, B, C, D, E, F** and **G**; e.g. 'the natural notes'.

Notation — the written representation of music, by means of symbols (music on a staff), letters (as in chord and note names) and diagrams (as in chord illustrations.)

Note — a single sound with a given pitch and duration.

Octave — the distance between any given note with a set frequency, and another note with exactly double that frequency. Both notes will have the same letter name;

A 220   A 440

Open chord — a chord that contains at least one open string.

Pitch — the sound produced by a note, determined by the frequency of the string vibrations. The pitch relates to a note being referred to as 'high' or 'low'.

Plectrum — a small object (often of a triangular shape)made of plastic which is used to pick or strum the strings of a guitar.

Position — a term used to describe the location of the left hand on the fret board. The left hand position is determined by the fret location of the first finger, e.g.
The 1st position refers to the 1st to 4th frets. The 3rd position refers to the 3rd to 6th frets and so on.

Quarter note — a note with the value of one beat in $\frac{4}{4}$ time, indicated thus ♩ (also called a crotchet). The quarter note rest, indicating one beat of silence, is written: 𝄽 .

Repeat signs — in music, used to indicate a repeat of a section of music, by means of two dots placed before a double bar line:

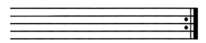

In chord progressions, a repeat sign ⁄. , indicates an exact repeat of the previous bar.

Rhythm — the natural pattern of strong and weak pulses in a piece of music.

Riff — a pattern of notes that is repeated throughout a progression (song).

Root note — the note after which a chord or scale is named.

Scale Tone Chords — chords which are constructed from notes within a given scale.

Semitone — the smallest interval used in conventional music. On guitar, it is a distance of one fret.

Sharp — a sign (♯) used to raise the pitch of a note by one semitone.

Simple time — occurs when the beat falls on an undotted note, which is thus divisible by two.

Sixteenth note — a note with the value of a quarter of a beat in $\frac{4}{4}$ time, indicated as such ♬
(also called a semiquaver).
The sixteenth note rest, indicating a quarter of a beat of silence, is written: ♯

Slide — a technique which involves a finger moving along the string to its new note. The finger maintains pressure on the string, so that a continuous sound is produced.

Slur — sounding a note by using only the left hand fingers. (An ascending slur is also called a 'hammer on'; a descending slur is also called a 'pull off.')

Staccato — to play short and detached. Indicated by a dot placed above the note: ♩

Staff — five parallel lines together with four spaces, upon which music is written.

Syncopation — the placing of an accent on a normally unaccented beat. e.g.:

$\frac{4}{4}$ 1 >2 3 >4 $\frac{3}{4}$ 1 + >2 + 3 >+

Tablature — a system of writing music which represents the position of the player's fingers (not the pitch of the notes, but their position on the guitar). A chord diagram is a type of tablature. Notes can also be written using tablature thus:

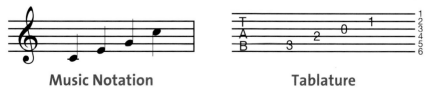

Music Notation   **Tablature**

Tempo — the speed of a piece.

Tie — a curved line joining two or more notes of the same pitch, where the second note(s) is not played, but its time value is added to that of the first note.

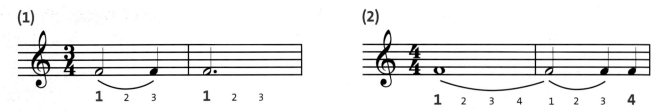

Timbre — a quality which distinguishes a note produced on one instrument from the same note produced on any other instrument (also called 'tone colour'). A given note on the guitar will sound different (and therefore distinguishable) from the same pitched note on piano, violin, flute etc. There is usually also a difference in timbre from one guitar to another.

Time signature — a sign at the beginning of a piece which indicates, by means of figures, the number of beats per bar (top figure), and the type of note receiving one beat (bottom figure).

Tone — a distance of two frets; i.e. the equivalent of two semitones.

Transposition — the process of changing music from one key to another.

Treble — the upper regions of pitch in general.

Treble clef — a sign placed at the beginning of the staff to fix the pitch of the notes placed on it. The treble clef (also called 'G clef') is placed so that the second line indicates as G note:

Tremolo (pick motion) — a technique involving rapid pick movement on a given note.

Triplet — a group of three notes played in the same time as two notes of the same kind.

Vibrato — a technique which involves pushing a string up and down, like a rapid series of short bends.

Wedge mark — indicates pick direction; e.g: V = down pick,   Λ = up pick

Whole note — a note with the value of four beats in $\frac{4}{4}$ time, indicated thus ○ (also called a semibreve).